ISBN 978-1-331-55708-1
PIBN 10205534

1 MONTH OF
FREE
READING

at
www.ForgottenBooks.com

By purchasing this book you are eligible for one month membership to ForgottenBooks.com, giving you unlimited access to our entire collection of over 700,000 titles via our web site and mobile apps.

To claim your free month visit:
www.forgottenbooks.com/free205534

Similar Books Are Available from
www.forgottenbooks.com

In Perils by mine own Countrymen.

THREE YEARS

ON THE

KANSAS BORDER.

BY

A CLERGYMAN
OF THE EPISCOPAL CHURCH.
(John McNamara)

"What judgment shall 1 dread, doing no wrong?"

MERCHANT OF VENICE.

New York and Auburn:

MILLER, ORTON & MULLIGAN,

NEW YORK : 25 PARK ROW. AUBURN: 107 GENESEE ST.

1856.

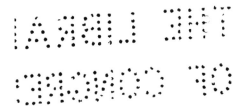

Edward O. Jenkins,
PRINTER AND STEREOTYPER,
No. 26 Frankfort st., N. Y.

DEDICATION.

[iii]

AUTHOR'S ADVERTISEMENT.

WHILE the following pages were going through the press, sedate old friends remarked to me, that the subject of which I treat, is too grave to admit of the levity which is often displayed in the narrative. The only reply which I can make to this is, that my book is a record of facts. The style is my own, the material was furnished on the Border. The scenes through which I passed were, in some respects, supremely ridiculous, and must be laughable; there were others which were inhuman, and must therefore excite horror. To write of events in any other manner than that in which they occurred, would not be a true history.

If the reader will be watchful, he will discover, that in those chapters which will perhaps be regarded by him as the most humorous, Miss Pussy is let out of her confinement!

NEW YORK, Sept. 5, 1856.

CONTENTS.

THREE YEARS

ON THE

KANSAS BORDER.

CHAPTER I.

INTRODUCTION.

THE writer of the following pages was a Missionary of the Protestant Episcopal Church, in that section of the State of Missouri called the Platte Purchase, during the years 1851–'2. This field of labor gave him every opportunity to learn the character and sentiments of those who have made themselves prominent in the late exciting drama in Kansas.

While he resided in North-Western Missouri, there was but one hope *expressed* with reference to the "coming in," as it was termed, of the Territory which lay on the other side of the river—it was to come in as Free Territory.

In the year 1853, he was invited to a charge in the city of Chicago, and accepted it. It was during his residence in this city that the Kansas Bill was introduced into Congress, designed to break down a barrier

1*

to slavery extension, which the Borderers never dreamed of. He was conscious of this fact, and was constrained publicly, at the time, to petition, with others,
against the measure. He was not *alone* in the Church,
as was supposed, in so doing. The late lamented
Bishop of New York, with several of his most influential clergymen, petitioned, with many others of our
Church, against the bill.

The hopes held out by the Kansas Bill made the
people on the border wild. The names of many with
whom he was familiar, he saw mingled with those
prominent at public meetings of an exciting and daring
character. He became much interested in the fate of
the Territory. He sought to go there, but not as a
partisan. He was recommended by the Bishop of the
North-West to the Committee of the Domestic Board
of Missions for an appointment to Kansas Territory as
a Missionary of the Church. The appointment was
made and accepted in the summer of 1854.

Several motives impel him to give to the public a
relation of personal adventure and experience during
his residence on the border, a period, on the whole, of
about three years.

The only criticism which can annoy me, will be to
prove the falsehood of any important statement made
in the body of the work.

Some of my friends tell me that those who do not
know the author will regard the *relation* of the whole
as fiction; these friends are correct, there is nothing
fictitious about the work save the *relation*, and this of
course is the author's prerogative.

CHAPTER II.

THE greater part of my furniture having been sold at public auction on Monday, the 2d day of October, 1854, I packed up those most necessary articles for comfort in a new country, and consigned them to a house in St. Louis. My wife and a pretty infant daughter I took with me to the cars, to leave at 11 P. M., for St. Louis. During the night it rained excessively. The car in which we were seated was thrown off the track. There was much confusion, but no person was injured. We were obliged, after long delay, to crowd ourselves into other cars, and leave the one which was off the track, behind us. Our lovely little babe received a cold during the exposure of the chilly night, from which she never recovered. We reached Alton late on the afternoon of Tuesday, October 3d. We changed from the cars to the steamboat which was to take us down the river to St. Louis. While on the passage, in the dusk of the evening, we had the vexation to meet the steamboat Polar Star, bound for the Missouri,—I had telegraphed to her Clerk from Chicago to reserve a state-room for my family. But our delay by cars frustrated our hope of taking advantage of this arrangement. I learned afterwards that the state-room had been kept for me until the last minute.

[11]

When we arrived in St. Louis, a city in which I was not altogether a stranger, I found our babe much worse. We took rooms at the Monroe House. In the morning I procured a physician for the babe. He did not think there was any cause for alarm. We remained in St. Louis two days on account of our child. I met one or two of my brethren in the ministry. The Bishop was absent on a visitation of his Diocese. Several of the laity called, and wished us "God speed."

We took passage on board of the then splendid steamer F. X. Aubrey, for Weston, Mo., on Thursday, October 5, at evening. We left in hopes that the child was much better. The water was unusually low on the river, and we advanced very slowly in consequence. Both my wife and myself were too much occupied in solicitude for our child to take any pleasure on the trip. We made no acquaintances on board, until the child became so alarmingly ill as to excite the sympathies of the officers and passengers. We experienced the utmost degree of kindness at the hands of all. To the Clerk of the steamer, and to Dr. Ruffin, of Lexington, Mo., I feel under great obligation. All our efforts, however, to save the life of the child, were vain. It died on the morning of the 9th of October, at 1 o'clock. We were just below the Baltimore Bar, twelve miles below Lexington. We reached the bar, and it was soon discovered that the boat would have to be "sparred over." This process occupied thirteen hours. The reader can well imagine my anxiety to reach Lexington with the body of my babe. The weather during the day was warm. I was almost distracted, lest I should see the tender flesh of my child show decided indications of decay before I could obtain a metallic case. At one time we searched the boat for material wherewith to make a coffin, but could find none. There was a very common and frail box, having potatoes then in, which I at one time in despair meditated taking, and, placing the body in it, bury it on the bank of the river! But at this moment of time the Genoa, a boat of lighter draft than ours, came in sight behind us. I could hardly doubt but that she would at once get over the bar. I went in haste to the clerk, and asked him if I could leave the boat with the body and go on board of the Genoa. He told me at once that I could do so, but added, that the G. would not get over before we did. He was right. I went on the forward promenade deck of our boat; at this time the Genoa had got close behind us. I discovered on board of the Genoa, Major Rich, sutler at Fort Leavenworth, and *once* a friend of mine. I hastily wrote a line and threw it on board of the boat to him, telling him my situation and requesting that if he reached Lexington before we did, that he would send the note to the undertaker, that he might have a metallic coffin at the Levee when we arrived. He replied that he would oblige me. Major R. retired, and in a few minutes returned accompanied by Major Macklin, paymaster at Fort Leavenworth, and *once* a friend of mine. We had not met for eighteen months. But in the meantime a Kansas Bill had passed which allowed a remnant of Barbarism to be extended—a feature in the Bill which he knew I disliked as much as it pleased himself. A few cold words of salutation passed between us. My destination was inquired with interest.

I will close this paragraph with the relation of a *faux pas* which, in the simplicity of my heart, I once made at Fort Leavenworth, in conversation with Major Macklin.

Major M., and family, at Fort Leavenworth, belonged to that class in our church, who revere the name Catholic. I was early taught what this sacred name meant. At the time of which I write, the usual debate had occurred in the New York Diocesan Convention with reference to the admission of Saint Philip's African Church, and its delegate, into union with the Convention. Major M. was anxious to learn my opinion about the matter. In the impulse of the moment, I concluded that his love for consistent Catholicity would be greater than his prejudice for color against color, and I said, how can they keep the church or delegates out on Catholic grounds? " Take care, sir! Many a fine prospect has been dashed by an unwise remark." Thus replied Major M. We never after talked together on the subject, or any of its cognates. This occurred two years before the passage of the Kansas Bill.

CHAPTER III.

WE got over the bar before the Genoa did, and reached Lexington about nine o'clock at night. I ran up into the town, while the boat lay at the Levee, in search of the undertaker. He had gone either a hunting or fishing, and his office and warehouse were closed. Oh! what was my agony. I hurried down to the boat. Told my wife to remain on board and go to Weston, while I took the body of my child and wrapped it in the linen of the bed, took it in my arms, and alone left the boat. The boat bell rang off. I took my seat in the carriage, and was driven to the hotel. A poor Irish woman had also a seat in the carriage. "Take care, sir," said she, "you will hurt the head of the baby, on the corner of the seat." I burst into tears, and sobbed, "No, I will not hurt it." "Ah, is it dead!"

> "Many a word at random spoken
> May soothe or grieve a heart that's broken."

The proud and enlightened Catholic, Major M., to preach the Gospel to whom I had risked my life, on the Missouri, at Fort Leavenworth, passed me by on the deck of the steamer,* with my dead babe in my arms,

* The Genoa reached Lexington immediately after we did. Major M. came on board of our boat. He never sought us out or inquired for us.

[15]

while the poor stranger, and ignorant Roman Catholic, wrung my heart with her sympathies.

When we reached the hotel, I asked for a room well ventilated. The poor negroes served me well; better than their masters. One went and got me ice. I inquired at the office of the hotel whether I could find a vessel to put the ice in, and lay the body on it. I was turned over to the negroes in the kitchen. The cook was interested at once, told me I might take anything that I thought would do. I selected a large copper boiler, and placed the ice in it, and laid the body on it. The negroes came, with the little ones, to look at the pretty white child. Thus they kept coming and going until late at night, when I was left, as I desired to be, alone, to watch the body and guard it from the many rats which infested the house.

The undertaker came during the night. He had no metallic cases. He suggested a coffin of zinc, and that to be placed in a well-made wooden case. These were ordered. I did not know at what time a boat might come up, and I was anxious to have all things in readiness should one arrive. Very early the next morning I awoke a Daguerreian, and told him that I wished to have a likeness taken. He prepared to oblige me. I took a negro boy to aid me in carrying the copper boiler, with the body, over to the artist's room. The picture was made to my satisfaction, when the boy aided me to carry the boiler with the body to the tinsmith's, to be sealed up forever from my eyes.

I felt much relieved, though in tears. I now waited two days at Lexington for a boat, but none came. At midnight, I understood, a stage would leave for Independence, which I resolved to take. The coffin was strapped on with the baggage! and I rode on all night, and arrived at Independence the next day. Here we telegraphed down the river, to learn whether there was a boat coming up. We could hear of none. I took the stage once more for Liberty, in Clay County, Mo. Here I found that there would no stage leave under three days. I remained there all night. Liberty is the home of the famous A. Doniphan, who led the Missouri regiment such wonderful marches in Mexico. I had the honor of his acquaintance, but he was not at home. From Liberty I telegraphed several times, and at length learned from below that the steamer Sam Cloon would be up during the night. I took a conveyance and went down to the landing, three miles distant, and lodged at a little inn on the river bank. The next morning it was raining; and at seven o'clock the Sam Cloon blew her whistle. I went on board. I found the boat laden with immigrants for Kansas, and others merely on a prospecting tour.

I had hoped now that in twenty-four hours my journey would be at an end; but what was my dismay, when I learned that the boat had been injured in her passage up, and that she would not go further than Kansas City. It was soon discovered, on board the boat, who I was, and the object of my journey to Kansas. I found several gentlemen from New York, Philadelphia, and one from Baltimore, who has since become famous in the territory. The destination of a part of the gentlemen, I was informed, was "Council Grove."

I knew where it was, and gave them some information. They seemed gratified. I was told by their
leader, that he was not a member of the Episcopal
church, but that he knew several of his company
were. He took my name and future address in the
Territory, and expressed the earnest wish that I
might visit their settlement, which has since been
named Council City, and has been made a missionary
station of our church. Had I at that time thrown myself into the hands of the Free State settlers, I might
have effected some good, and saved myself many
troubles; but I had many intimate and kind friends
among those who were slave-holders in Missouri, and
I wished to labor not among them, but in their neighborhood, only across the river.

The Sam Cloon reached Kansas City a little before
noon, on Saturday, the 14th October. She could go no
farther. We were now forty miles from Weston. We
must perform this journey by land. The only conveyance which we could procure was a lumber wagon,
and a very frail old buggy. The coffin was fastened
on behind the buggy, and one or two ladies and a
driver seated themselves inside. Three men and myself
took the lumber wagon. We crossed the river to the
Missouri side, and began our journey on a pretty cold
afternoon. We reached Parkville, in Platte County,
about eight o'clock in the evening, and took supper.
We then left for Weston, twenty-eight miles distant.
We passed through Platte City, the home of David
Atchison, about 1 o'clock, A. M. We were so numbed
with cold that we were obliged to halt and kindle a fire.

When we had become comparatively comfortable we left for Weston, seven miles distant, and arrived at four A. M. of Sunday morning, the 15th October. I went directly to the hotel, the St. George, where I found my wife, waiting for me most anxiously. I went at once to the sexton to have a grave dug. I owned no lot in the grave-yard. I told him to dig for the present in that portion where they buried strangers. Many a prodigal son is buried there, far away from their once happy homes! The grave was soon dug. I went to tell a friend, a physician, of my loss, and asked him to come with me to the grave. The solitary carriage took my friend, afterwards a member of the famed Kansas Legislature, my wife, the body, and myself, to the grave at the break of day, and there I consigned the sweet child to the tomb which it had long sought for. The father was the officiating clergyman! There was none other of our church in the place, and I would have my child buried by none other service than our own.

CHAPTER IV.

WESTON, though not the County-seat, is yet the chief town of Platte County, Mo. Taking all things into consideration, it is an important place. For many years it remained the only town in the vicinity of Fort Leavenworth. It was consequently the immediate resort of the free and easy soldier, after pay-day at the garrison. I need not describe the condition of his finances, or the fancies of his brain, the day after the Fair! The officers' families did most of their marketing and trading at this place. The Quarter-Master threw millions into the coffers of the traders at Weston, and the farmers and stock-raisers of its neighborhood. The streets and shops of the town, two or three times in the year, would be crowded with the various tribes of Indians, who would have come to trade after receiving their payments. In addition to all these means of gain, much of the over-land trade to New Mexico, California, Salt Lake and Oregon, took its rise from here. The traders of Weston, in a word, did an immense business. I never was in a town of 2,800 inhabitants, in any State, where money, in gold and silver, was so plenty, and where wealth was so general in the possession of the traders.

Beside these circumstances, Weston had a character

[20]

for men and measures, peculiar even in Missouri. Here was published the " Platte Argus," the organ of David. Atchison: here were the Committee Rooms of the famous " Self-Defensives:" here the fate of Empires was decided by an oath : here a Southern Confederacy occupied the minds of conspirators : here civil war was prayed for as a blessing: here B. F. Stringfellow smoked his pipe and plotted treason to the Constitution: and here Parson Kerr took his drink, quoted texts in support of Barbarism, read his doggerels burlesqueing philanthropy, and printed speeches advising bloodshed.

CHAPTER V.

THIS was the name of the chief Hotel at Weston. We remained at it about a month. It was filled to overflowing at the time, with lawyers, speculators, and politicians. Here was a knot of some half-dozen persons, eagerly listening to a very fluent Dr. F—— descanting on the many advantages of situation and resources connected with Marysville, one hundred and fifty miles interior, on the Big Blue, Kansas: a rude pen-and-ink draft of the future city was displayed by him, and small portions of copper ore exhibited, and declared to abound close by the city-limits. Shares in the town held at $100 each. In like manner the praises of Leavenworth were cried aloud. Four hundred dollars a share, but no title guaranteed. Every shareholder must enter into bonds to help to secure the title, *i. e.*, to help to rob the Delaware Indians of their land!

Bills announcing the completion of the survey at Kickapoo City, were thrown in at the door—a sale would at once be made. Wonderful advantages at Kickapoo City—" Fortunes ahead!" " *Fortes Fortuna juvat.*" Coal-beds underlie the city! The deepest water on the Missouri is at this place! It will become the outlet of Salt Creek Valley! No humbug about

[22]

the title! Hurrah for the future Emporium of Kansas! "Walk up, gentlemen. John Ellis' flat-boat will be in waiting to take parties across at 11 o'clock.'

P. T. A., the President of the Atchison Association, chaunts the glory of "Atchison," a new town at the mouth of Independence creek, to be the future home of Davy the Immortal. All the Mormon immigration would outfit there!

"Pawnee, Pawnee!" shouted a shrewd little lawyer • and speculator—a little-great-Benton-man, and a sore thorn in the side of David.

"Pawnee, Pawnee, at the head of navigation, on the Kansas, near Fort Riley, the point selected by the Governor for the capital of the Territory."

These towns and fifty more, had their advocates at the St. George. Men were going out and coming in constantly, with rolls of foolscap in their hands, having charcoal sketches of future cities thereon. They reminded me of students on a commencement-day, with their orations in their hands, flitting about the college-buildings. The tall cotton-woods of the Territory are in sight from the hotel, and a few poor straggling Kick-apoo Indians look in amazement at the white men violently gesticulating and pointing with their rolls of paper towards the Territory, lying in its primitive state. Poor Kickapoo, take up your traps and go cut forty miles farther—they are selling your little corn-patches and the sites of your wigwams. The very burial-place of your fathers has been this day sold in town lots, with the bodies therein laid, without the contemplation of removal. The lots would not have been

taken as a gift, on such conditions! The bell rings!
The voices are hushed for a moment. The rolls of
paper coil up instantly, without an effort on the part
of their holders; they are placed carefully in their
hats, and the crowd rushes to the dining-room. The
bustling multitude help themselves, and when the edge
of their appetite is taken off, a few murmurs or
whispers are heard in my neighborhood! "The Episcopal preacher has got back! How does he stand on
the '*goose?*'" Strange cabalistic! I had to learn
afterwards what it meant!

CHAPTER VI.

THEN AND NOW.

Two years before this visit, when I was the aceredited Missionary to Weston and St. Joseph, I was told that I was *very popular !* When I first arrived, a lady from Baltimore, since departed this life, canvassed the town for nearly a month, soliciting funds to purchase a lot for an Episcopal church. She succeeded, but her success looked to me very much like failure. She wept at her many rebuffs, and at the misrepresentations of her motives. Notwithstanding these things, which I thought looked ominous, I was much courted and feasted. Several weddings, to which much eclat was attached, I had the honor of solemnizing. The bride, on one occasion, a pretty Miss of fifteen years, a day or two before her marriage, while passing the door of her lady friend, at whose house I was staying, said, " Mrs. P., fetch along your little preacher, *I* am going to be married in style !" She was married in style ; her father, Elijah C., furnished the champagne without limit. The first volley of corks numbered the years of the bride. At this salute I retired, I hope, with honor !

Mrs. P., before mentioned, was a sister of one of our bishops. She was a Christian and a member of the church. She owned a negro man who wished to get married to a Miss Cecilia, a negro girl belonging to Mrs. D. Frank must go and ask Mrs. D. whether he could have Cecilia. Mrs. D. rather hesitated. Poor Frank besought her in the most pathetic terms, for his lady-love. "Ah! now, Miss D., dear, do let me have her, I shall die if you don't!" The heart of Mrs. D. was won. Now the question was, when, and how, and by whom they were to be married. Mrs. P., Frank's mistress, told him that I must be got to marry him. "Ah, Miss Ginny (the lady's name was Virginia), I can't have your preacher, because he charges so much!" Mr. P. brought Frank up-stairs to my room. Frank addressed me very respectfully by name, and inquired when I would next hold service in the church. I wished to know why he was so anxious. He turned his cap over and over in his hand, and picked at it for a moment or two, without answering me. His master had to come to the rescue. "Frank is going to be married," said he. "Why, Frank," said I, "what do you mean?"

Frank was very black, I could not discover that he blushed, but I think that he felt a glow in his face, at any rate he showed teeth which a duchess might have envied.

"Well, Frank," said I, "you want me to marry you. Who is the happy one to be?" "Cicilly," said Frank, "Miss D.'s girl." "Well, I will marry you two weeks from Sunday next, at 2 P. M." "Well, sir, how much are you going to charge?" I laughed heartily, but poor Frank was much in earnest, I saw, and I told him that I would not charge him anything, as he occasionally swept out the little meeting-house at which we held service. Frank went off much pleased at the prospect of getting a good wife so cheaply.

The negroes made great preparations for the wedding. High life below stairs was to be illustrated. Frank and his Cecilia were much envied by the black folks. "Goin' to be married in 'Piscopal Meetin'." "There'll be no livin' with them, I reckon."

The eventful Sunday came. The *tin horn* blew for meeting, at 1 o'clock. We assembled, and the church was filled with the white congregation, and the service began. I had proceeded as far as the middle of the Psalter, when eight or ten couples, headed by the bridegroom and the bride, and the procession, followed by many stragglers, marched up the aisle to the reading desk. I was dismayed. What should I do? They were too early by three-quarters of an hour. I was much afraid that the whites would think that I had arranged this matter intentionally, and I at once stopped in the service, married, and dismissed the party. An old Englishman growled out his displeasure, "that I had condescended to marry them at all, much more that I had permitted such parade!"

Another instance will go to show the general favor in which I once stood. There was living in Weston a young lady, as famous as the renowned Sally Ward. Rose W. was the sister of a noted Salt Lake and California trader. There could be no gala-day in the famed Platte Purchase, unless Rose W. was the Star of the "Dramatis Personæ." When the Missouri River Packets laid up to remain all night at Weston, the chief clerks, as soon as the boats touched the levee, would travel post-haste and vie with each other to gain the gracious response of "I will be there," from the "Belle of the Border." The announcement would be made. "A dance on board the Isabel, the Clara, the Ben West, or whatever might be the name of the fortunate boat,—and Rose W. will be there!" Rose had been really "engaged" fifty times, but the community would exaggerate, for it had Rose off to be married a thousand times. Rose never left her home for a day, but it was said she had gone to be married!

At this time I resided at St. Joseph, thirty miles from Weston. A letter reached me saying that my services would be required on such an evening to marry Rose W. It was put into my hands by the stage-driver from Weston, who laughed as he performed the action. I recognized the handwriting of one whom I knew would respect me more than to trifle on such a matter, otherwise I should have treated the affair as a hoax. I felt satisfied that "the wolf," in the shape of a bridegroom, had caught Rose at last. The intelligence created some excitement in St. Joseph, however; none would believe it until I should have returned and told them on my honor that "the knot had been tied."

The horse stood saddled for me on the day previous to the wedding, and I started for Weston. When I drew up at the livery, the heads of the young doctors, lawyers, and clerks were protruded, some smiled others laughed equinely, but most looked blank despair, for they felt that their Cynthia was in good earnest about to withdraw her beams from them forever.

I went to the rooms of the bridegroom, and there I

learned that the brother of the bride disapproved of the marriage. This was opposition from an unexpected quarter, and even at this late hour I had fears with reference to the result. Several committees of conference were held by the friends of the "young people," to no purpose. The bridegroom, on my recommendation, went to Rose and put the question, "Shall the marriage take place, the veto of your brother to the contrary, notwithstanding?" She answered,—"placet." I found that I had a *two-third* constitutional vote in favor of the marriage, and as the parties were both of age, I married them. I fancy that John C. Fremont would have been glad to have had my services on a similar occasion.

"The Belle of the Border" was refused a wedding-party by her brother, but a rich treat was got up at the rooms of her husband. The wife of her brother attended and assisted. All the carriages and buggies in the neighborhood were in great requisition. Large premiums were offered for a horse. Multitudes came to town from the country. Horns were blown, drums were beat, guns were fired, bonfires were lighted, and yells were made by the crowd for the appearance of the bridegroom. He was obliged to throw out the coin, that the crowd of the uninvited might have wherewith to make merry. The sounds of revelry ceased:

> " The harp that once through Tara's halls
>   The soul of music shed,
> Now hangs as mute on Tara's walls
>   As if that soul were fled."

A day or two after the wedding, the trunk of Mrs.
P., late Rose W., was opened, and there were found,
among other trinkets indicative of her personal charms
and of the estimation in which she had been held, two
bundles of cigars, and forty-eight Daguerreotypes, the
likenesses of her rejected suitors!

Neither of these parties were connected with the
Episcopal church; I must be allowed, therefore, to
think that a non-resident Episcopal clergyman having
been chosen to perform the ceremony, indicated a
choice on personal grounds.

Still, these circumstances and the like, furnish the
interesting episodes in every clergyman's life. I would
by no means have it inferred that I enjoyed one round
of halcyon days during my first sojourn in the Platte
country. It was often my privilege, after a journey
of thirty miles, to "sweep out and dust the room," in
which service was to be held on the morrow—and to
carry out the ashes and make the fire on the Sunday
morning. The regular fare between Weston and St.
Joseph, by stage, I had, by a personal interview, com-
muted to one-half; and this sum, in the aggregate, for
one year, I paid with funds not received from my parishioners. My raiment, unlike that of the Israelites,
waxed old, and an exchange was never effected
through the liberality of the people, except in the
single particular of a pair of inexpressibles, furnished
by one who has lately become by election, a Free State
Attorney-General. I can illustrate what I would have
understood on this head, by a remarkable case in point.

While I resided at St. Joseph, in 1851, the California fever had not ceased to rage. The infection had even spread to the ranks of the preachers. It will be borne in mind that St. Joseph was the "jumping-off place;" in other words, it was here the emigrants bade farewell to civilization and entered upon the long journey through a savage wilderness.

I was sitting in my study one morning, when I heard a footstep on the stairs, and in a moment afterwards a modest knock was given on my door. I gave the *entre*, and a very fine specimen of a gentleman stood before me. He held in his hand a large sole-leather hat-box. He blushed slightly, while I asked him to take a seat. "I called this morning, sir," said he, " on what you may regard and what I feel to be, a strange errand." So saying, he fumbled in his vest-pocket and found the key to his hat-box. He opened the box and took out a worsted muffler, about a dozen of half-worn shirt collars, and as many, perhaps more in number, of white jaconet neckcloths, and a book published by the Appletons, entitled "Five Hundred Sketches and Skeletons of Sermons." Said he, " Sir, I learn that you are the only person in town who wears white neckcloths, and I wish to dispose of these, together with the accompanying articles! I am going to California." I did not know what to reply— I perceived that the man was in his senses, and I hesitated. He guessed the thought which was passing in my mind, and inquired—" How are you sustained here?" "Oh, so, so," said I. "There is but one story," said he, "in answer to my own inquiry. My story is the tale of nineteen in every twenty of the ministers

of Christ, of whatever name. I have been, sir, a minister of the Presbyterian church in Virginia for the last
fifteen years. But I have been ever in a condition
worse than a beggar; I have been kept in debt. I
have been fawned on and flattered. Told often what
a fine sermon I had preached, and what an affecting
prayer I had made. I was constantly invited out to
dinner or to tea, but I could put no *l'argent* in my
purse to pay my rent, get me fuel, or bread for my
family. I am now on my way to California, and I
wish to sell out the insignia which appertain to the
priest's office." I did not know which to do, laugh or
weep. I purchased his stock—the book I retain yet,
the hat-box was sold at auction, with other matters, in
Chicago, and the neckcloths have long since become
as threadbare and as holey as will be found in the ward-
robe of any parson whatever. This very true story
will illustrate the condition of my affairs in days gone
by, in Weston and St. Joseph; I had a smile from
everybody—I could go to tea or to dinner anywhere,
or I could have with pleasure a carriage to take a ride
when the owner did not intend using it himself. But
now how changed!

Now, a heart-broken mother is landed solitary on
the levee at Weston, while her husband is on his sad
journey behind her with the dead body of her babe;
she takes her rooms at the hotel, and waits, with awful
suspense, for six days, his coming, but not a call of
sympathy is made by the once parishioners of her husband, who had for many months preached to them the
Gospel of Christ without money and without price.
Times change, and we change with them.

CHAPTER VII.

WHEN I had been absent from Weston and St. Joseph some months, having accepted a call to Chicago, Illinois, in 1853, I received a letter from the Rev. W. N. Irish, then Rector of a parish in Columbus, Ohio, making particular inquiries with reference to the condition of things at Weston and St. Joseph. I replied in as encouraging a strain as I thought was consistent, and referred him, for further particulars, to the Bishop of Missouri. The result of all was, that, very early in the spring of 1854, the Rev. Mr. Irish found himself installed in my late charge at these towns. I had never had the honor of a personal acquaintance with my reverend brother. He had concluded to make his home at St. Joseph, and officiate at both points, as I had done.

While at the St. George Hotel, in Weston, I received a call from him, the nature of which I must now disclose. He had come down from St. Joseph, and driven to the house of General Stringfellow, in Weston. In about an hour after his arrival, he came and introduced himself, with a smiling countenance, in the parlor of the hotel. I was very glad to see him. I believe that he is about the same age with myself, and, if memory serves me well, we took orders about

2*   [88]

the same time.   We were, therefore, more likely to be
social, and on a par with each other.   We met on
ground every inch of which we both knew well.

There were some two or three persons in the parlor
at the time.   Mr. I. asked me at what points in the
Territory of Kansas I would officiate.   I told him the
letter of my appointment read, "Fort Leavenworth,
and parts adjacent."

" You can't preach at Fort Leavenworth," said Mr. I.

" Not at the garrison, I know; but at the town outside," I replied.

The bill organizing the Territory located the seat of
government at Fort Leavenworth—(this was afterwards altered)—but I was under the impression that a
town would be founded near that post.   Mr. I. told
me that " he had organized a parish, called ' St. Centu-
rion,' at the garrison, and that, as soon as practicable,
it would be transferred to Leavenworth City."   I remarked that it would then come under my care.   He
smiled at my simplicity; and then went on to tell me
the many favors which he received at the hands of
Major Maclin's family: he added, that he would visit
the Major in the morning.   I asked him to do me the
favor to present my regards to Major M. and his family.   I was then asked if I would not accompany him
to the garrison.   I told him no; that I had seen Major
Maclin, on my way up the Missouri, and that he had
not invited me to visit him at his quarters, as he had
ever done in times gone by.

After Mr. Irish had returned from his visit at the
garrison, he called again at the hotel, and imparted to

me the information that Major Maclin had said that, if I called at his quarters, he would treat me with respect; but that he would never invite me there. This settled the matter. Mr. Irish went on to inform me, that I would receive instructions from the Domestic Committee in New York, charging me to keep perfectly quiet with reference to the Slavery question! I was thunderstruck.

Mr. Irish," said I, "which side do you take in the matter?"

I am well satisfied," replied he, " that Kansas will become a Slave State."

"Did you ever hear me say that it would not become such?"

" No; but you protested against the passage of the Kansas-Nebraska Bill, while you were at Chicago."

" So did," said I, " Dr. Wainwright, the Provisional Bishop of New York, and the Chairman of the Domestic Committee, whose forthcoming instructions to me you now anticipate, and forewarn me of." I went on to say that, the Committee being composed of clergy and laity, it could not, according to the genius of our Church, instruct a clergyman with respect to his doctrinal teaching, or otherwise, save in matters of mere form. The Committee, I acknowledged, had the prerogative to make representations to my Bishop, and that he could admonish ; and that, Bishop Kemper being my Bishop, his godly admonitions and counsel I would always respect.

" Well," said Mr. Irish, " the instructions will come in some shape."

"It is a bad rule, sir, which will not work both ways," I replied. "If I cannot be allowed to express a hope that Kansas may become a Free State, which is to be my future home, I cannot discover by what good fortune you are to escape instruction, when you evidently feel satisfaction at the idea of its becoming a Slave State, while your home is the State of Missouri. We are both in the employ of the Domestic Board of Missions."

He saw, at once, the absurdity of his position, and he changed the subject.

"Well," said he to me, "I am going to officiate at Fort Leavenworth whenever I can, and also at Atchison. I would advise you," he continued, "not to go to Atchison; you will be insulted if you do."

This was beyond endurance. I told him that he must keep within his own mission, and labor within the jurisdiction of his own Bishop. That the Territory of Kansas was, for the present, my exclusive field. He softened down considerably, and I revoked the above, and told him to do all the good for which opportunity might offer within the Territory. He remarked to me that he "dare not invite me to preach for him." I presume that this stands without parallel in our Church.

Not many weeks after this interview, it was published in the journals at St. Joseph, that the Rev. W. N. Irish would deliver a lecture, entitled "The Religious Sentiment in Henry Clay's Writings." An eulogistic editorial notice was taken of the lecture, and particular commendation given to a passage, in which the reverend gentleman had given a scathing rebuke to those ministers who protested against the repeal of the Missouri Compromise. Two weeks after this, it was announced in the papers at Weston, that the lecture would be repeated in the Methodist meeting-house. It was repeated; our boarding mistress, who was a slaveholder, and my wife, went to hear it. I declined going.

The eloquent passage was repeated: "I am not one of those clergymen who protested against the passage of the Kansas-Nebraska Bill." The inference which all drew was: "There is such 'a pestilent fellow' in your midst."

Many months after these events, I received signal charity in great sickness at the hands of my Rev. Brother, for which I can never be too thankful "Amicus Socrates, amicus Plato sed magis amicus veritas."

CHAPTER VIII.

WE had remained a month or six weeks at the " St. George Hotel " In the meantime, as will hereafter be explained, I had made diligent search for a house on the Kansas side of the river, but was unsuccessful. There was a family in Weston, highly respectable, to which I had been recommended to seek a boarding-place for my wife, during the winter. My wife was in very delicate health, and required much nursing care. The principal persons in the family above alluded to, were two aged females, a mother and a daughter, and both were widows. The mother was upwards of eighty years of age, and quite feeble ; she has since died. The daughter was over sixty years of age. She had three sons in California, and one who resided with her. The two widows owned between them ten negroes, five or six of whom lived at home. Mrs. O., the daughter, and manager of household affairs, was a remarkable person. I have rarely met with a female of such sound, practical good sense ; or of such enlarged views upon vexed questions in the State. The family was from Lexington, in Kentucky ; they had been playmates of the "Sage of Ashland." I understood that this Mrs. O. was desirous of securing a small family to dwell with her, for the sake of the society which would in such case be afforded. With the prayer in my heart that God would prosper my errand, I went to seek as great a favor, I considered, as I had ever asked from any of my fellow-creatures. I approached the house with a palpitating heart. I knocked on the door, and was admitted by Mrs. O. Her mother was sitting in her easy-chair by the stove, a withered leaf! Her mental abilities were not much impaired, however. Mrs. O. was a lady of imposing appearance and manners. She was tall, but not fleshy. Her hair was a very dark brown—she wore spectacles. I made known in very modest tones the object of my visit. I perceived at once, that there no prejudice existed against me. It appeared that through her daughter, who had died during the year that had just passed, she had conceived a favorable impression of me. We had met in society in past days. There was nothing, therefore, to be settled but a purely business matter. The rooms which were to spare were shown me; I was more than satisfied; indeed, I would have gone into the kitchen, had that been the only place of refuge. Mrs. O. desired to see my wife before we could close our agreement. She was gratified in this respect, and, it appeared, more than gratified with the interview. We felt at home, and we were at home. Mrs. O. made me her confidant and adviser in many of her worldly concerns. Her favorite son returned from California, and she was pleased to introduce me to him as her "dearest friend." "Praise the Lord, O my soul, and all that is within me, bless His holy name." I had found in God "a hiding place from the storm." "In the shadow of thy wings will I make my refuge until these calamities be overpast." We were now settled in the family. I have before said that there were five or six negro servants in the house. There were two grown negro women, one man, and several half-grown boys and girls. We treated them kindly, but we had been accustomed to the proper regard which was paid to them by their mistresses, and never, by word or deed, intimated that their condition was not a good, and perhaps the best, one for them. I never felt inspired to render the negro slave discontented with his lot. I saw and could appreciate the evil of slavery on both classes of the community, the masters and their slaves, but it is an *overpowering* evil. Vain is the help of man! May God help both parties most interested. Man must not foster and entail this evil on the posterity of new and future empires. We cannot do so without sin!

We were in this family now in comparative peace. I found that I could leave my invalid wife with these good ladies, and their servants, while I was absent in the Territory on duty. "But in the midst of all this peace the tempter comes." "He comes in the shape of a woman, to turn this paradise into a hell." Mrs. Stringfellow, and another lady, whose name I have forgotten, called on Mrs. O., to inquire "If she was aware that she was harboring Abolitionists?"

This Mrs. O. related to me herself. She told them that she was "competent to judge of the character of the inmates of her family!" These ladies, and many others, discontinued their social calls on Mrs. O., after this time.

CHAPTER IX.

"THE SELF-DEFENSIVES."

THIS was the name of a famous Association of Pro-Slavery insurrectionists at Weston. It embraced the inhabitants of the County of Platte, who, on being examined and approved, were declared "sound on the goose," received the benediction of Parson Kerr, U. S. A. chaplain at Fort Leavenworth—the right hand of fellowship from B. F. Stringfellow, and Peter T. Abel, the Nimrods of Abolition hunters—the mark in their foreheads from Dr. George W. Bayless, Surgeon-General of the army of Kansas Occupation—the sacramental oath of a true knight of the Manacle of Slavery, from David R. Atchison, Vice-President of the United States!

This Association has had but one parallel—the famed Jacobin Club, in France, with Robespierre at its head. The persons whose names are above-mentioned, occupied seats " *in summo penetrale Tonantis*," they constituted the power behind the throne. Good-natured old A. J. Galloway—Father Galloway—was the *apparent* chairman of the Society, and Perry Wallingford was the secretary; not so guileless as Father G., but a chief among good fellows, and beyond suspicion "on the goose." Dr. George W. Bayless, a gentleman of great respectability in Platte County, three miles from Weston, and the same distance from Platte City, was an active member of the Self-Defensives. He was a member of my vestry when I had a charge at Weston. I considered his house my pleasantest place of resort; the green spot in the desert. He is a gentleman of refinement, rarely to be excelled, of superior education, and of exquisite taste. He has at his place a splendid conservatory of rare plants; and this feature is not a *purpureus pannus*, but in perfect keeping and consistency with all around him.

It is quite common to hear said, that the decent people of the border disapprove of the outrages in Kansas. I must think that George W. Bayless, and B. F. Stringfellow, the very first among the first of the first families of Virginia, feel greatly complimented! "Save us from our friends."

George W. B. rises to debate!

"Hear, hear!" roar the belted knights of the "Self-Defensives."

Could "the goose" speak, it would say: O, all ye faithful in "gooseology," take George for an example —his faith must be sound whose conduct's in the right. O, ye adepts in gooseology, beware of that vilest of all heresies, Solifidianism—"faith without works is dead." Free-soilism and Abolitionism "still live!" "The Union yet stands." Remember the words of the apostle of South Carolina (hear, hear)— "When I hear a Southern man cry: 'The Union, the Union is in danger,' methinks I snuff treason on the tainted gale." "In conclusion, hearken unto George, and show your faith by your works." Three cheers were here given for "the goose." When the applause had subsided, George W. B. offered the following resolution :

"That we, the members of the Platte County Self-Defensive Association, do solemnly pledge ourselves to go at the call of our brethren who are across the river, in Kansas—(here George gave a sly wink, and said, 'They will surely call us.' Cries of 'They will')—and drive out from their midst the abolition traitors." Here were deafening cries of "Question—question."

Father Galloway rose. Poor old man, let him be forgiven—he knew not the import of that Resolution. The cape of his old dragoon coat trembled on his shoulders, as he rose to inquire "if they were ready for the question." "Question—question!" shouted the chivalry. "All those who are in favor of the Resolution just offered by Dr. Bayless, will say aye." "A–Y–E." No man dare say no, so the noes were not called for.

> "The thunder ran from pole to pole,
> Olympus shudders, as the thunders roll."

The crowd of mortals in the streets of Weston, those who lived by the public, were mightily alarmed at this hubbub among the gods, and they had a meeting forthwith, and passed resolutions, inviting immigrants to come, as they had heretofore done, and buy goods in Weston. The names of those who signed the call for this meeting may now be seen, within a gilt frame, in some of the public places of Weston.

CHAPTER X.

" A horrible thing had been committed in the land.'

THE Rev. Frederick Starr was the minister of the New School Presbyterian Church, in Weston. He had labored with much diligence for seven years in this, perhaps the most discouraging field in our country. He was a small, active, well-informed young man, about thirty years of age, perhaps. He was a graduate of Yale College. He was never weary in well-doing. His congregation, nevertheless, continued very small. The truth is, he was too faithful a man to conciliate such a community. Mr. S., however, labored along in faith, and with untiring energy. They called called him " The Yankee." It was often said that he was "too sharp"—that the man who would get round him must graduate in a "Yankee college," and take an " ad eundem" degree of "Master of Arts," in Kentucky. It is allowed on the Border that a Kentucky Yankee *"can't be beat."* " The Self-Defensives" resolved to issue a "quo warranto" against Starr. The inquisition was to sit with open doors, in the Presbyterian Church. Father Galloway was escorted to the pulpit! His official robe was that same old coat—the dragoon coat—light blue in color—bright buttons, with the glorious eagle of our common coun-

[44]

try stamped thereon, and the letters " U. S. A." Who could doubt his authority? Perry Wallingford, secretary, took his seat at the Communion table. The minutes of the last meeting of the " Self-Defensives" were laid on the table. The Rev. Mr. Irish took his seat in the body of the church. Dr. Bayless and Jack Vineyard, the great accusers, took their seats in front. Vast numbers of the citizens thronged the body of the church. The ladies were there, arrayed in all their furbelows on their dresses, and feathers in their bonnets. Their salts and their handkerchiefs were kept ready for application. Whispers were distinctly heard in all parts of the building. The City Marshal and his assistants were there, to keep order about the doors The light-haired, fair-complexioned, handsome little parson made his appearance. Fear had no place in his composition. He was summoned to the bar! Or, rather, to the pulpit of his own church. Several smiled at the unusual sight—Father Galloway in the desk, and Preacher Starr in the pew! The minutes of the last meeting were read and approved; the Resolution which summoned the Rev. F. Starr before them was then stated to be the order of the day! The reverend culprit came forward, and bowed his head.

The accusations were read. I think Jack Vineyard had this honor. There were three charges, which, if not explained, and the minds of the community disabused, expulsion from the County and the State was to be visited upon the accused.

The first charge was, that the Rev. F. Starr had taught the negroes to read. The second, that he had proposed to a negro man named Henry, to buy his freedom, and that he had been the treasurer and adviser of said Henry. Third charge, that the Rev. F. Starr had been seen riding in a buggy, in open day, with a " negro wench." There was quite a buzz among the ladies on the announcement of this charge. Father Galloway shook his sides with laughter. Mr. Starr, himself, smiled, while an oath or two were heard at the door. There were decided indications of a break-up, but that would never do. " The Self-Defensives" must not have their authority impugned or ridiculed· The accused must reply to these charges.

> " Perhaps it would turn out a song,
> Perhaps turn out a sermon."

Father Galloway informed Brother Starr that he was permitted to speak for himself.

Thanks were returned for this privilege, and the preacher defended himself, after the manner of Paul before Agrippa.

He reminded the people how long he had been with them. That no man had lost a servant by his instrumentality. That he had never intimated to a negro that there was a better state for him than that of slavery. That no servant in town or country, had become discontented, indolent, or disobedient to his master or mistress, through any fault of his. None of these statements were controverted. He came, then, to the charges. The first was, "that he had taught negroes to read." He plead guilty to the charge, but showed, in defence, that in every case where he had done so, he had had the written permission of the master.

"The country is going to the devil," cried Jack Vineyard, at this statement.

The parson replied that the owner of the slave could give such permission, and that the permission was a sufficient indemnity for the teacher. Something was grumbled out that he might employ himself better than to teach negroes—"That, sir, is a matter of opinion," replied Starr. With respect to the second charge, "that he was the treasurer and adviser of Henry the negro," who wished to buy his freedom, he also pleaded guilty, but showed that it was all satisfactory to the master of Henry. He came now, he said, to the third and last charge, and confessed that in this particular he would be obliged to throw himself upon the mercy of the "Self-Defensives." (Tremendous sensation, and cries of "No, no!") Father Galloway laughed again! Cries were made for the ladies to retire. Mr. Starr at once perceived that he had been misunderstood, and called on the crowd to listen. "Order, order!" shouted Father Galloway. Mr. Starr went on to explain, that to the third charge he had not the decisive rebutting testimony similar to that he had advanced to the previous charges. He said "it was true that he had ridden in a buggy with a negro servant, but how this could be construed into a crime he could not comprehend." He was answered, "that criminality was not charged. It was the fact itself— that it was highly improper in his particular case, as he was generally supposed to take too much interest

in the class of negro servants—that it had a tendency
to insubordination by making the negroes think that
they were as good as their masters" Mr. Starr said,
" that it was quite a common circumstance to see servants riding in the same vehicle with their masters
and mistresses, and even to have them sit behind them
on horseback. As well," said he, "might you arraign
the children in the street for playing with a negro
child."

On motion of Dr. Bayless, the charge was dismissed.

The Rev. gentleman was now asked to give his
opinion on slavery in the abstract. He declined doing
this, unless they would declare that nothing which he
might say would ever after be brought forward against
him. After some discussion this was decided in the
affirmative.

Mr. S. then went on to say, "that he was a northern
man—that he had come to dwell amongst them and to
preach the Gospel of Christ, from an imperative sense
of duty; that he was a colonizationist in principle;
that on the existence of slavery in the abstract, he believed it to be morally and politically wrong! that
these were his honest sentiments; that they were born
with him, and nurtured and fostered by education;
that there were no northern men who did not occupy
the same ground; that it was impossible that their
sentiments should undergo a radical change in this
particular." At this stage of the proceeding the Rev.
W. N. Irish rose up, and begged Mr. Starr's pardon—
that there were exceptions—that he had been born

and educated in the State of New York and that during his residence in the States of Virginia and Missouri he had radically changed his mind." "Then, sir," said Mr. Starr, "it requires exceptions to prove rules, and you but illustrate and prove my position!"

The Rev. Mr. Irish, like the Sage of Kinderhook has earned what he has received from me, the character of "a Northern man with Southern principles." Dr. Bayless declared himself satisfied with the defence of the Rev. Mr. Starr. The case was dismissed. But as often happens, so in this case, the man who has been once put on trial can never rid himself of *a suspicion.* The Rev. Mr. Starr was in a few months afterwards waited on by a committee and decidedly ordered to leave without any "*ifs or ands.*" He left, and I believe is now settled somewhere in the neighborhood of Rochester New York.

CHAPTER XI.

AN ABOLITIONIST SOLD AT AUCTION.

THERE was residing at Leavenworth City a lawyer by the name of Phillips. He was very decidedly in favor of the Free State interest. His decision of character, popular talents, and position, gave him considerable influence. He had been oftentimes publicly abused; at one time he had been seized by a mob at Leavenworth, but was rescued by his friends, who were driven to desperation by the act, and who seized every weapon which came in their way likely to aid them in defence. The great hatred by which the Pro-Slavery-ites were actuated towards Phillips at this time, was accounted for from the fact that he had made an affi-davit to the effect that the election at Leavenworth City for the members of the Legislature was fraudulent. It was in consequence of Phillips, and others, that the election was declared void by the Governor, and a new suffrage to be taken. The curses which were given to Phillips were both loud and deep. Particularly was the organ of the " Self-Defensives," the " Platte Argus," published at Weston, exercised against him. An elec-tion on the border was a matter of no small interest. The chivalry, like Cæsar of old, had crossed the " Rubicon," *alias*, the Missouri: their dispatch to the

"Platte Argus" ran : "We came, we saw, we con-
quered."

Thus they did, and returned home. What was their
dismay when they found a Yankee Lawyer bold enough
to run up and spike their gun! The charge of the
light brigade at Balaklava was child's play compared
to this! "The Platte Argus" now had work before it.
Everything was to be done over again. It had to set
a tune for these lines :

> "He that fights and *runs away*,
> May live to fight another day."

"The Platte Argus" generated, and shot its lightning,
and rolled its thunder weekly against the cowards of
Leavenworth City. When its battery would be too
highly charged with electricity to hold in a week, it
was obliged to let off in "extras" against the devoted of
Leavenworth! "The Argus" "doubted whether there
was a true friend of 'the goose' in Leavenworth." "If
there are any of the faithful there, why is the traitor
Phillips permitted to live!" It continually harped
against "the Leavenworth Herald." "The 'Herald'
must not call itself the advocate of 'the goose' while
that traitor Phillips lived in the same town in which
it was published."

"The Herald" would weekly whimper out its meek
apologies, and say a word about "circumstances over
which it had no control!"

But, "no whining, gentlemen," replied "the Argus."

"The Herald" saw the plight in which it was placed.
When it took up the "gray goose quill," it dreamed

of the freedom of the press, but it awoke, and behold it *was a dream!*

Come, "Mr. Herald," stir your stumps, the Diplomats of the Army of Occupation in Kansas "The Weston Regency," the "Self-Defensives" are after you with a long pole! Give an account of your stewardship.

Wm. Rives Pollard and Wm. H. Adams, editors of "The Herald," asked each other what they should do, for, of a verity, their lords were about to take from them "the stewardship."

Wm. Rives Pollard was named after a gentleman, and *looked like* a gentleman; he wore magnificently large ruffles in his bosom—a distinctive badge of the F. F. V.'s.

"I tell you what we will do," said each to the other, "let us *betray* Phillips to cross the Missouri; we shall have the tar and feathers all ready for him on the Missouri side." "We will strip him, over there, on the solitary river-bottom, clip his hair off, coat him with tar, and apply the feathers. We shall then ride him on a rail through the streets of Weston, while a drum shall be beaten, and the chivalry will cry out 'victory,'" which, you know,

"If *not* victory, is yet *revenge.*"

"And every body praised the Duke,
    Who this great fight did win."
"But what good came of it at last?"
    Quoth little Peterkin.
"Why that I cannot tell," said he;
"But 'twas a famous victory."

All that the editorial corps devised was carried into effect. Phillips was enticed over the river. They did to him all that was desired. He was brought to Weston in that awful plight. They cut off the hair of his head, but his strength did not fail him—he was a Samson still. His body looked contemptible, but the soul of the man was there; they could not tar and feather that!

Col. Lewis Burns now approached him, and tried to wheedle him to sign a paper declaring that he would leave the Territory of Kansas.

"No, sir," said the hero, "I am in your power, you can put me into the Missouri, if you please, but I will not voluntarily leave the Territory!"

A negro was now brought forward, and commanded to sell Phillips at auction.

"How much, gentlemen, for a full-blooded abolitionist, dyed in de wool, tar and feathers, and all?"

Laughs and jeers followed this sally of humor on the part of Sambo.

"How much, gentlemen? He will go at de fust bid."

A quarter-of-a-cent was bid, and Phillips was sold!

Phillips returned to Leavenworth, but the editorial corps dare not go back for some days, the indignation at Leavenworth was so great against them.

The Mayor of the city of Weston called a meeting to consider the steps, if any were to be taken, with reference to the disgraceful proceeding. The Mayor declared that he would resign, if such riotous conduct was approved by the citizens generally. A large meeting was held, and a most exciting debate took place, but the proceedings were finally disapproved of by the majority of the people.

This mattered little to the editorial corps. The "Platte Argus" endorsed the " Leavenworth Herald;" it was declared sound on the "goose." The right-hand of fellowship was once more extended to them. Their late magnanimity had covered a multitude of sins. The Virginia ruffles on the bosom of Wm. Rives Pollard might at any time be inspected at the office of the " Platte Argus," after this auspicious day !

CHAPTER XII.

A PENNSYLVANIA LAWYER PEDDLES BEEF; BUT TURNS OUT A HERO!

I WAS one day riding in a buggy with a Dr. F., of Weston, from Fort Leavenworth to Weston. The mud in the roads could be measured by the foot. Soundings had to be taken by us as we drove along. While in the midst of our troubles, a spectacle presented itself. A queer-looking, dried-up little man on horseback, with a child in his arms, was plodding his weary way towards the Fort. He was followed by a female, also on horseback, with a child in her arms! I could not help smiling at the sight. I concluded that such people had an object before them in life! They were surely in search of something—"the bubble reputation" in a quagmire in Kansas. I asked Dr. F. who they were, as I observed that he recognized them with an inclination of the head. The Dr. was surprised that *I* was not acquainted with the "Prince of Traitors, McCrea!" "Is that McCrea?" replied I. "O, doctor, you give me too much credit for intimacy with the sayings and doings, and the heroes of the Free State movement." "Well," replied the doctor, "I must acknowledge that there is little to be laid to your charge, and I think that I understand you better than the most of them at Weston." But this is digressing. I had heard of McCrea, but I had never seen him before. The hero of my imagination had now dwindled into a pigmy, and that pigmy in a plight! First impressions, first impressions, said I— alas, alas! I perceived that philosophy was about to fail me, and I tried to ransack my brain for historical personages whose personal appearance bore no resemblance to the nature of their actions. I had read Homer, and I had a dim recollection of a hero mentioned by him, " Whose little body encased a mighty mind." This reminiscence had the magic effect to take the child out of McCrea's arms, remove himself from off the jaded, drabbled horse; it stripped him of his mean clothing, it trimmed his hair and his beard, it arrayed him in the " *Toga virilis*," or the manly gown of the ancient Romans, gave him the dignity of a Senator (I mean a *Roman* Senator), the boldness of Demosthenes when he harangued against tyranny— finally, it put a pistol in his pocket to defend the liberty of speech!

Every Squatter meeting which might be called in the neighborhood of Leavenworth, McCrea would be at. Squatter Sovereignty meant something in his vocabulary, whatever it did not mean at Washington. McCrea was forever tacking provisos and amendments to the Squatter laws and resolutions, to the great annoyance of the pro-slavery catspaws of the wire-working " Self-Defensives." These suggestions were always designed to secure fair play to the Free State settlers. There were many Free State men in the neighborhood, and McCrea knew it; but very few of them pursued any aggressive policy—they were afraid of blood-shed! But McCrea feared nothing in the shape of a man. His enemies gnashed on him with their teeth. He was branded as the "Prince of Traitors, or Aboli-tionists"—" The Agent of the Emigrant Aid Society,' and so on. McCrea had to do something for a living, as a matter of course. He was a lawyer; but as there *was no law* in his neighborhood, there was, of course, nothing for him to do in that line. He stuck up his " shingle," " McCrea's Law Office;" but this was to keep up appearances merely, and to establish a reputa-tion for the harvest in the " good time coming." Should anybody now have called at the office of the "*Juris Consult*," his wife would have told the person that her husband had gone out to "peddle beef!" Fresh meat was quite a luxury, I can tell my readers. As a beef-peddler, McCrea was decidedly popular! He drove his wagon over to Kickapoo City, about six miles from Fort Leavenworth. The cry of " Beef, beef!" spread like fire on a prairie through the town. Men, women and children were seen fleeing from their houses, as if they were fleeing from the yawning earth at the time of an earthquake! The wagon was sur-rounded. Part of the beef was sold, and all were cry-ing for their share, when one came up who cared more for the " goose " than he did for beef, and cried " Aboli-tionist." McCrea told all hands to leave the cart, threw the cloth over the beef, and closed the sale! They besought him in vain. His principles had been assailed, they could have no more beef. He drove off amid the yells of the crowd!

*

But McCrea did not give himself up altogether to beef-peddling.

Squatter meetings were looked out for as eagerly by him as ever cat watched for mouse. When the "spirit" of the "Self-Defensives" *came up* to trouble the waters, McCrea let no man get before him, to step in! A great movement was set on foot at Leavenworth, which was designed to cut off all hopes from the Free State men. McCrea, the evil genius, was the first on the ground. Many resolutions and noisy debates were offered, and held. McCrea moved, and had the good fortune to have seconded, a resolution, the exact import of which I am not now able to give; but, no doubt, it was on his darling subject—protection to Free State squatters. It nettled the crowd excessively. Malcolm Clark, a very good fellow when not crossed in his plans, rushed on McCrea, in fury, with a club in hand! McCrea retreated as far as I understand the law in Pennsylvania requires, in order to justify the last resource, armed self-defence—drew his pistol, and shot Clark dead! The crowd rushed on McCrea, who dashed into the Missouri river; the mob seized him; preparations were making to hang him, when the dragoons from the garrison rescued him, and put him in the guard-house, at the Fort. McCrea, after some months' confinement, awaiting trial, escaped.

CHAPTER XIII.

My letters of appointment gave me Fort Leavenworth and parts adjacent as my field of labor. I will speak of Leavenworth City in another chapter. Kickapoo City lies adjacent to Fort Leavenworth—improvements were earlier made at this point than at Leavenworth. The population was as large in number for a long time. I found my prospects better at this place than at Leavenworth. The first newspaper in the Territory was published close by the town limits—" The Kansas Pioneer," still issued from Kickapoo City. In addition to all these things, it was nearer to Weston, where my wife boarded. I could easily walk the two or three miles which intervened between the two places, and preach on Sunday.

The first sermon which was ever preached to the whites on this ground, I delivered, at the old log-house called the " Roman Catholic Mission of the Kickapoo Indians." The files of " The Kansas Pioneer" will show this, as this fact was very emphatically stated by the editor, in a number of the paper.

There was quite a large number of persons present. The subject of my sermon was : " What shall it profit a man if he shall gain the whole world, and lose his own soul." This text suggested a train of argument

[59]

very suitable to that community; quarrelling and contending, as the people were, about claims and town
lots. The editor of "The Kansas Pioneer" was there
—his name was Sexton; indeed, the paper was printed
and published under the same roof which covered us
while preaching. I did not ask the editor to notice
my sermon, or the circumstances under which it was
delivered. He did so, however; but he never did it
again. It was whispered to him, from some source,
that I was not sound on the "goose"! I made an
appointment for the next service to be held in two
weeks. I had purposed giving the next to Leavenworth City. When I returned, to fulfil my engagement, I was met by the Missionary of the Kickapoo
Indians, who remarked to me, "I suppose that you are
aware that I have made an appointment to preach for
the whites, to-day?" I told him that I was not at all
aware of it. He had never done so before, and never
would have done so, had I not made appointment there.
This old gentleman belonged to the "Methodist Episcopal Church, South." He could not read a chapter in
the Bible more correctly than most children of ten years
in our common schools. His name is N. T. Shaler.
He was sound on the "goose;" consequently, the log-
house, which had now passed, by *conquest*, into the
hands of the whites, was offered to him to preach in,
and denied to me! I would not postpone my service,
but went to the house of one of the citizens, whose
sentiments on the "goose" were like mine own. We
had a very small congregation. I officiated, and returned to Weston. If any other sacrifice had been

asked of me, than to postpone my service, I would have made it. I saw the trap which was laid for me, very plainly. But now they had got a slight pretext to injure me ; and the most was made of it.

"The Kickapoo City Association" had passed a resolution that any religious body might, by its agents, select a lot in the town, on the condition that such and such a building should be erected thereon in the course of eighteen months. The "Self-Defensives," individually, had a large interest in this town, and it is amazing to me that there was not coupled with the conditions, that the religious body should be sound on the "goose." But this was an oversight such as the farthest-sighted cannot always guard against. I went and claimed the lot—selected it, and had the certificate made out. I was much encouraged at this success; I had got a foothold. But, bless you, talk about footholds! when you had "Self-Defensives" to deal with! However, I went to an old friend of mine, sound to the core on the "goose," and sent to the Legislature without opposition. Said I, "Doctor, you are going to live at Kickapoo; I have got a lot for our church there; do get up a subscription, and for *every dollar* that you get subscribed and paid, I will add one to it, and we shall have a church built at once." The doctor took the bait. He disliked the old Kickapoo missionary. The subscription was got ready in a week or two; the sums subscribed amounted to $350. But the doctor pocketed the subscription, and I never could get him to explain to me why he did it. I think that I can account for it in a future chapter.

I continued to preach regularly at Kickapoo City in the private house of William Braham, a settler, from Michigan City, Indiana. He had a wife and two children, a son and daughter. Many and many a time did the wife weep over her loneliness, and the many petty persecutions which she endured because her husband had the misfortune to be appointed a justice of the peace by Governor Reeder! To add to her afflictions, and to remove her only companion, her daughter of fifteen years died! I attended that sad funeral. The accustomed sympathy of the neighborhood was not extended to that heart-broken mother. I ventured once to say to a friend of mine in the street of Kickapoo— "You and others ought not to treat poor Braham's family with such neglect." "He is a villain, sir," was the answer! Braham's family had been educated in our church, and their children had been baptized in the church—it was really the only family on whom I had much claim, in a spiritual point of view. I would not neglect them on any account.

Under the caption of this sketch, I must mention that Mr. Sexton, the first editor of the "Kansas Pioneer," and who baptized it to *advocate bloodshed*, became converted under the pious ministry of Parson Shaler, has since entered the ministry of the Methodist Episcopal Church, South. I understand that he is a *burning*, if not a shining light!

CHAPTER XIV

TWENTY-NINE BED-FELLOWS AT LEAVENWORTH CITY.

I WALKED down to the city of Leavenworth on a Saturday, in the middle of November, 1854. It had been announced that I would preach there on the following day. Everything was bustle and confusion. There were many notables there on that Saturday. A. J. Donaldson, Marshal of the Territory, was there; Mr. Woodson, Secretary of the Territory, was there that day; John Calhoun, Surveyor-General of the Territory, was there that day; Judge Johnson was there; Judge Fleniken, candidate for Congress, was there that day; Martin F. Conway, who came with indorsements from the best démocrats in Baltimore and New York, was there that day; Major Macklin and Major Ogden of the army, were there that day; and many other lesser lights were there that day. What brought all the talent together there that day? I will tell it here, though I hope that it will not reach the eyes or the ears of Manypenny, Commissioner of Indian Affairs, Caleb Cushing, Attorney-General, or even Jefferson Davis, Secretary-at-War. Many of the above-named had come to attend a meeting of the Leavenworth Association. This association had laid off a town, on lands not subject to pre-emption. They had been warned by Commissioner Manypenny and Caleb Cushing, and gently catechised by Jefferson Davis. The town is either laid off on the " Military Reserve," and therefore not subject to pre-emption any more than the lands on which Pawnee was laid out at Fort Riley, and decided by Jefferson Davis to be given up—or it is laid off on Delaware Indian lands, not subject to pre-emption, but to be sold to the highest bidder for the benefit of the poor Indians. Take which horn you please, gentlemen, you are all interlopers! So the most of these gentlemen were down at Leavenworth to-day on a speculation! Yes, gentlemen, you were all fishing in forbidden waters to-day. Governor Reeder was removed for giving a *quid pro quo* to the Indians for a few hundred acres away in the interior of the Territory. Officers in the United States army were allowed to wear the uniform while they continued to buy and sell that which belonged to the Indians, and that which belongs to them to this day, in the most important section of their country. Oh, shame shame!

But the most of the speculators have departed. Many have gone to their homes, *i. e.*, to their snug quarters at the garrison. Many of them have gone to Weston. I could now see who were likely to be on hand to-morrow. Pennsylvania was pretty well repre-sented. There was Doctor Lieb, who must figure in a chapter " all alone by himself." The doctor is worthy of this distinction. I will just here observe that the doctor had not the least objection to balance a tumbler in his hand, and say, "My respects, sir," and then apply the instrument to his lips, and allow the contents to pass them, as if they were *used to it!* Let this be borne in mind, for the doctor will appear in another character by-and-bye. I thought at first that I should have the honor of the doctor's presence on the morrow at service, but he informed me that he was the "guest of the Moravian minister, Mr. Smith, missionary among the Delawares." I could tell.better, as night approached, who were likely to be at service in the morning!

The notice of the service came out that day in the "Leavenworth Herald;" it had circulated at the garrison, only a couple of miles distant. I knew that there were several very high church communicants there—perhaps they would be down. I had seen Major M. among the speculators—surely he will be down on the morrow. I consoled myself with the reflection, that the long walk of eight miles would not be in vain—that I would not have to pay my two dollars per day at the hotel, and no good to accrue from it! When the supper-bell rang, it called in quite a crowd, and I had great hopes for the morrow. They looked like men of energy, but I could not tell decidedly; they operated lustily at table, but I would not allow myself to estimate according to this rule; for I have often been forcibly persuaded that the laziest men will manifest much energy at their meals, and show a disposition to carry away with them heavy burdens; but, I suppose, if they should be expostulated with, they would say that the burden was not "grievous to be borne!"

The Leavenworth House," at which I was stopping, was a house, to the extent of just having the "balloon

frame" up, and cotton-wood clap-board-siding nailed
thereon. There was neither lath nor plastering thereon. We did not have to take a candle in the morning,
to look for daylight! Daylight sought us out through
a thousand holes, in the morning! But, no anticipa-
tions. We are at supper—which was a good deal like
other suppers, under like circumstances. In a few un-
important items, the supply exceeded the demand.
Potatoes loom up, now, in the imagination of my reader; but he is mistaken—they were, at that time, three
dollars per bushel. No; the items consisted of long
strips of fat side pork, swimming in what they call, in
New York, "soap fat." The items wherein the demand
exceeded the supply, consisted of a little pickled cab-
bage, pickled cucumber, dried apple-sauce, and some
biscuits, which the knowing ones were satisfied contained some flour in their composition. Every man, as
he rushed to the table, laid one hand on the back of
his chair, and, with the other, stretched over and selected the morsel suited to his taste—"there is no
accounting for tastes;" three actions were performed
at the same moment of time—the chair was seized,
the man sat down in it, and the delicacy found itself
grasped beyond hope of escape. It exploded the notion at once, that the mind cannot guide and direct several actions of the body at the same instant.

There was a general laugh among the successful ones;
while the rest selected their piece of corn bread, and helped themselves to the pork. They must have read "Jacob
Faithful," and profited by the example of that philo-
sophic boy—" Keep cool."   " Better luck next time."

After supper, many of the men liquored at the bar, and procured cigars. I forgot to mention that the room which we were in was bar-room, dining room, smoking room, whittling room, sitting room, standing room, coughing room and spitting room, reading room and writing room, committee room and debating room. After the cigars got well lighted, the house, almost unconsciously to itself, dropped into a " Committee of the Whole on the state of the Union, and on the state of Kansas in particular." There was no secretary formally appointed by the meeting; but I thought that, this being the "Gibraltar" of Kansas, I would just quietly vote myself into that office, for the sake of posterity; we all owe something to our *anterity*, and I think we must place posterity under obligations to us. At least, so I thought on the present occasion. I will, in the first place, mention, that almost every State and Territory in the Union had a worthy representative. There was a son of the Granite State who knew Franklin Pierce from the time he was a boy. I think that he said that he went to school with him. "But, la!" said he, "nobody thought that he would ever become great!" Here, a fellow from New Mexico wanted to know if the expectations of Frank's friends had been agreeably disappointed? He went on to give a rather stale account of the fainting fit which the Brigadier had on the field of battle; but it was not listened to with any relish. Another, from Mississippi, related some youthful frolics which he had in company with Jefferson Davis. He seemed to agree with Col. Benton, that Jeff. was "one of them." Another recollected the *time when* Marcy *bought* the inexpressibles, which, in after years, created so much discussion in polite circles. This was taken down by the listeners, as Tom Benton said he would swallow the Cincinnati Platform, with the proviso that it be brought up by a stomach-pump, or some other more forcible process. They looked at the wrinkles on his horns, and perceived at once that he was too young to have remembered " When those old pants were new."

Several prognostications were made with regard to the course of policy which would be pursued by the President and his Cabinet with reference to Kansas affairs. Each had an opinion according to the *personal* knowledge which they had of the different members of the Cabinet. Some were hopeful, others desponding. Most were disposed to wager their money on the war-horse from Mississippi; they declared that State, Interior, Law, and War, would all be attended to by Jefferson Davis—that the affairs of the "goose" were safe in his hands. The house was not divided on the question; the above was a foregone conclusion.

The house resolved itself now, by tacit consent, into a " Committee of Ways and Means." Lucian J. Eastin, occupied the Committee with a few remarks, in which they were all personally interested, viz.: How a title to the land at Leavenworth City was to be secured. Said he, " however much I may write about the certainty of securing a title, in my paper, the 'Leavenworth Herald,' there is some doubt about it! (Hear, hear.) In a paper, you know, we write a great deal for buncombe (laughter), but to those who are initiated there are no secrets. The next House of Representatives, I feel well satisfied that Jefferson Davis cannot manage. The Delaware Treaty, therefore, will not be altered (hear, hear, and sensation). This is my candid opinion." Lucian resumed his pipe. An attorney by the name of Rees, delivered a long argument, reviewing the opinion of the Attorney-General, Caleb Cushing, on the Delaware Treaty. The other members of the Committee acknowledged that the argument of their Committee-man, Mr. Rees, completely riddled that of the Attorney-General, but for practical purposes it was useless. If Jefferson Davis could not manage the next House of Representatives, then it was all day with them. This seemed to be the general opinion.

Several gentlemen, who had wisely kept themselves in the back-ground, and in silence heretofore, now ventured to show how long their ears were. These gentlemen seemed to have been *purchasers* of "shares in Leavenworth City;" they were not of the *original stockholders*. These poor simple ones had heard a magnificent scheme spoken of, which would remove all difficulties. A million of dollars were to be raised by the original stockholders, and with this sum Wall street itself should be outbid on the day of sale! I glanced my eye searchingly at the foreheads of these gentlemen, and I observed some peculiarity in them quite similar. I concluded that the bump of Causality, together with that ridge directly over the eyes, under which is said to reside the perceptive faculties, had been too closely and too pointedly examined by the digits of their loving and ambitious mammas, when their craniums were too susceptible of impressions being made thereon! Perhaps it will be better understood, if I should say, when their foreheads were as pliant as a newly-laid egg!

The other members of the Committee, who were original stockholders, here winked at each other, as much as to say, "allow these gentlemen to enjoy the luxury of this happy hallucination!"

Several other members of the Committee told of their experience in such things. They called the attention of the Committee to the way in which they did things at Fort Snelling (hear, hear). I observed, myself, that this was talking to the point in debate. I glanced at the craniums of these old-stagers, and what was my surprise! I rose from my seat to take a bird's-eye view of their crowns, when lo! there were discovered protuberances on each like unto the horns of calves, when they are about four months old! I was now satisfied that "blood and fire and vapor of smoke" would mingle largely in these gentlemen's remarks. I was not disappointed. Fort Snelling was dwelt on with gusto. They had attended the sale there. Their pistols and their bowie-knives held in their hands, and they would liked to have seen the man that would have dared to bid more than one dollar and a quarter per acre for the land! (hear, hear, and cheers.) Fellow Committee-men, said they, we throw out these remarks, hoping that when the hour of need comes, they will not be forgotten. Some two or three Yankees turned pale at these remarks, but they will get used to it if they remain long enough. The Committee began now to drop off one by one—finally there was no quorum present, and I asked to be shown up stairs.

I was shown up to *the bed—the bed* was all before me where to choose! The room up stairs was the same size as that which we had just left below. It had not been partitioned off; nor had lath or plaster been used. The windows were in—the floor was laid temporarily—the boards did not lie close enough together to be tight. There was not a bedstead of any shape or kind in the room! We discovered blankets of every hue and texture, lying spread all over the floor—there were blue blankets, and red blankets—gray blankets and dirty yellow blankets; these latter had once been white blankets; but now they bore the color of the Missouri waters which were rolling past, a yellowish, muddy color. I say the *bed*, therefore, lay all before me where to choose, with the exception of that part of the bed already occupied. I counted noses, and discovered that there were *fifteen* already in the bed! There were two or three thoughts which flashed across my mind—I wished to get as clean a blanket as possible, and I desired to be as far removed from the rest of my bed-fellows as I could. I saw a blue blanket lying close up in one of the corners of the bed, *i. e.*, in the corner of the room; I hastened to it, as I heard the footsteps of more bed-fellows coming up-stairs—there were six in this last crowd—there were now twenty-two, including myself, in the bed—not all lain down, but all *in the bed!* I observed with satisfaction, that the last knot of bed-fellows did not show any disposition to crowd me. They laid off but one or two articles of their raiment, and each took their blanket and laid down, after having put their boots and coats where they intended to place their heads. If there were any prayers said by them, they were not repeated kneeling. In two or three of the acts of these gentlemen I imitated them; for instance, I merely laid aside my hat, took off my coat and boots, and put these under the place where I had selected to lay my head; I took the blanket and laid me down. Three more bed-fellows now came in—these made twenty-five. One remarked, it is going to be cold to-night; yes, they all agreed that it would be cold; the wind was changing to the North. These two or three came a little closer to me than any yet, but this was to be accounted for from the fact the bed was getting *full!* I felt the wind coming in around me, and I at once perceived that I had made a mistake in my selection— an *outside* part of the bed, and that part of it which lay towards the North! I now perceived why I had the corner to myself, and my right there was none to dispute. It was quite late when the balance of the twenty-nine came in. I could not go to sleep on account of the cold. These latter gentlemen seemed quite anxious about their comfort—they asked each other, in an under-tone, whether their feet were more likely to be warmer with their boots on or off? There was no unity on the question; one of them came and took the candle or lamp in his hand, and then went back to where the rest stood. He whispered to them;

there was a smothered chuckle. I at once concluded that there was to be some practical joke attempted. The fellow who had the lamp walked softly, but leisurely and apparently unconcernedly, from one part of the bed to the other. He was taking observations! He was anxious to know how many stars yet twinkled in the plain before him! The lamp cast its beams near me, and I drew the curtain over my stars, i. e., I closed mine eyes! As I was the North Star, he seemed to take pity on me, and left me. My stars came from under the cloud as soon as he left me, and I blinked up just in time to see him removing as gently as possible, the blanket from off a fellow who had evidently gone to dream-land! One of his companions now took his turn with the lamp, and was equally successful; and so of the rest. These took their places in the bed, with two blankets each, and I have no doubt were soon comfortably asleep. The poor fellows who were robbed of their blankets began to grow weary, and one by one they awoke, and behold their blankets were gone! The name of a certain spirit and his dwelling-place were muttered with evident displeasure by them. They took the lamp and went a fillibustering! They made conquests, and returned evidently better pleased. Those whom they stripped awoke, and one of them made a terrible row. He was one of those in whom there was no joking, at least, he did not relish being the object of a joke. The whole bed was in a few minutes alive, a general reckoning had to be made. The four fellows who had each two blankets began to devise ways and means of getting rid of their extras, lest they should be called to account for that "night's uproar." An equal division was made, but all hands were now so chilled that sleep to the great majority was a thing impossible. A general conversation began and lasted till morning. There was a "great cry, but little *wool !*"

Preparations were made about the usual hour, for service. The blankets were all thrown into a heap together. The trunks and boxes which were in the room up-stairs, were drawn out, so as to afford seats—as many chairs as could be spared from below were also brought up—a little stand was placed for me to read from. All things being in readiness, I went in person to the tents of the people who were camped on the town site, and invited them to the service and preaching. Very many replied to me very respectfully, that they would try to be there; but as I left several of the tents, I heard roars of laughter! The little dinner-bell rang for meeting. The congregation collected. There were sixty or seventy men, and but two or three females. I read portions of Scripture, and then made some selections from the Service. I read the Litany entire. There was not an individual there who understood our Service!

I preached the same sermon as I had delivered in Kickapoo City, on the text, "What shall it profit a man if he shall gain the whole world and lose his own soul." The subject was just as appropriate there as it had been at Kickapoo. The people were quarrelling, and contending about claims, and lots, every day, with the additional reason, that they contemplated sinning yet more, in making every effort to cheat the Delaware Indians out of their lands! The service was now closed. I was anxious to know whether I could make another appointment. The keeper of the hotel said that he hoped, during the coming week, to have the room partitioned off, and plastered, and that in such case it would no longer be suitable for service. I dismissed the people without making, at that time, any appointment. The congregation went below; I remained up-stairs for some little time, arranging my papers, &c.

I have before remarked, that the floor of this room was but temporarily laid. There were spaces between the boards. The remarks of those who were below could be distinctly heard. It is said that listeners hear no good of themselves; but I heard Lucian J. Eastin, and another gentleman, talk in rather a *mixed* style; one said, "Fine preacher;" the other replied, "Yes, but not sound on the 'goose.'"

CHAPTER XV.

A VISIT TO BULBONI'S, IN THE POTTAWATAMIES COUNTRY.

A DAY or two after my visit to Leavenworth City, I was sitting in the office of Dr. Bonnifant, of Weston. While there, two Indians came in, belonging to the Pottawatamies; they had come from eighty miles in the interior, to get the doctor to go out and see their sister, who was lying dangerously ill. The terms on which the doctor would visit, were agreed upon; and he determined to go. I asked the doctor how he intended to make the journey? He informed me that he would go on horseback. I said he would be frozen to death; this was late in November, '54. I told him that I would like to go with him, if he would take a conveyance with wheels on, as I would like to see that portion of the Territory, and also learn what the future prospects for the Church might be. We proposed to hire a double team, and pay the expense between us. This was at once arranged. I hurried up to my boarding-place, and in a very few minutes prepared for the journey. When I returned to the office of the doctor, a superior span of large, gray horses were standing, ready harnessed, in a large Rockaway, before the door. Dr. Bower, the partner of Dr. Bonnifant, a real good fellow, and his own worst enemy, was bustling about to get a barley loaf or two, and some cheese, not forgetting a

[76]

"comforting flask" for the doctor. The Indians led the way in their buggy, and we were off.

This chapter has no special denouement; but it has got some notes, which a greater than myself, the renowned Mr. Pickwick, would have transferred to his journal with considerable satisfaction.

We soon reached Fort Leavenworth. Said I, "Doctor, just drive to the Sutler's office (wherein Uncle Sam's mail-bags were overhauled), I wish to see if there is anything there for me. "We drove up." When I had got within the door, I heard, as usual, the voice of Major Rich, Sutler, Postmaster, &c., delivering a lecture on his favorite subject, "gooseology." I went at once, without asking (which was a privilege every body had), to the dry-goods box, in which bushels of papers were, turned them all out on the floor, and then sorted them all back again, save those on which I found my name written. This process occupied some time. Meanwhile the lecture was going on. There were several officers of the garrison present, and a few civilians. The lecture, this morning, was addressed to Major Graham, I think, of the topographical corps, though on this point I will not be decided; at any rate, he was of the rank and file of the army, and, therefore, Major Rich's superior officer. But it was wonderful to note what deference was paid to the teachers of the new faith of "gooseology." Major Graham, in the meekest tones of voice imaginable, remarked: "But, Major, is it not lawful to talk about making Kansas a Free State —surely this is the right guaranteed by the organic law?" "Reeder, and his crew of Abolitionists, must be hung, sir." "But I cannot see why," said Major Graham. "Stop, stop, Major Graham, it is bad enough for you to get letters from Chicago!" He was post-master, and of course knew this *secret Evidence enough to hang a man!* Major Rich now came forward to me; I put out my hand in the blandest manner; this did not conciliate the Major. Said he, "Why do you not have your letters and papers sent to your own office?" "Oh," said I, very coolly, "I am missionary to the *whole Territory*, and I am found sometimes at one place, sometimes at another; my friends know this, and I am written to at Fort Leavenworth, Leavenworth City, Kickapoo, Mount Pleasant, &c." "Well, but where do you get the most of your mail matter?" "For the present at Weston, where my wife boards." The name of Weston seemed to bring to the recollection of the old gentleman many favors, and kind attentions, which I had paid to his mother-in-law, in times of great affliction. A favorite daughter had died, and left two orphan boys, the nephews of Edward Stiles, Esq., lately appointed Minister to Mexico. Before the new science of "gooseology" came into vogue, I had been anxiously pressed to take the charge of the education of these boys; but as I had not learned this science, which was to be a "sine qua non" in their education, I would be the last one thought of now! I took my papers and left. We were now on the road fairly. It was quite a pleasant day, the roads were excellent. We drove over the high, rolling prairies, and soon crossed the Stranger Creek, at Dawson's, a famous stock-raiser, and teamster, and contractor with the Government for carrying stores from point to point on the plains. "It is here, somewhere," said the doctor to me, "where that Minard lives, whom they shaved, and drove out of Weston, because of his unsoundness on the 'goose.' I'll be dog'd," said the doctor, "if it was not too bad. It was put to the vote," said he, "and carried by a small majority, that he should be shaved, and driven out of the town. He left, and is now living here." Yes, and he has defended himself, and his neighbors, during the late exciting and bloody times. We drove along over the prairies, not a house to be seen on either side of us. I felt a little qualmish —we were now actually *out at prairie;* I cannot discover any greater impropriety in saying out at prairie, than there is, out at sea. Those who have never been out at prairie, of course, will call it an absurd conceit, this. But travel, gentlemen, travel—take a trip to the Rocky Mountains, *now, at once,* for the sublimity of solitude will soon be gone! Leave old ocean till another time—he will wait for you; they can't "pre-empt" him; there is no corn to be raised in his foam.

We passed Charley Hart's, at Hickory Point; we shall visit Charley as we return. We drove on until we came to the crossing of the Grasshopper—here we purposed stopping all night. "Dyer's trading post" was here. The Indians went down to the creek, and camped. Our horses were put out, and a supper was got ready for us at Dyer's. It was a *second,* but *smaller* edition to that at Leavenworth City. The house was a very dilapidated old log. There were several apol ogies for beds, in the common room; bed-fellows of

the "genus homo," were not quite so numerous as they
had been at Leavenworth; but we had plenty of company, in the shape of little customers which love to go
in advance of, and with, civilization (if I am not mistaken, they browse upon man in his savage state);
they are thieves—they know well that they are unwel-
come visitors; they come at night, when all is hushed
save the snoring of some wearied hind, and insert their
probosces into the tender " leathern bottles," and revel
in the claret! but when chanticleer proclaims the
morning's dawn, they dance off to the sound of his
music, and pray for the cracks and the crevices, to hide
them from the wrath of the bipeds!

We were ready for the resumption of our journey
before daylight. We started, and when we reached
the Creek we found the Indians all ready. The whips
were applied to the horses, and we were off at full
speed. We were soon out at prairie again. We
reached Soldier Creek about noon; took out the remains
of our barley loaf, procured some water from the Creek,
and took a lunch. We gave the horses some water, and
started again. As we were driving through the woods
in the creek bottom land, I discovered a number of
Indians, perhaps thirty or forty, of all ages and sexes,
camping. They really looked wild to me. We did
not hear them say a word. It is surprising how un-
social the Indians are, unless they should have their
tongues loosened with whiskey. It was their silence
which overawed me. When we had passed them, I
could not help looking back through the glass in the
back of our carriage. Just simply to hear myself

talk, said I, "Doctor, two of those fellows are coming after us!" The Doctor felt for his pistol, a revolver, and looked out at the side of the carriage,—of course we both laughed that it was not so. We drove along and crossed "Cross Creek," and soon came in sight of the "Kaw Indian village," away seven miles distant, on an elevated bluff of the Kansas river. We drove along on the Kansas river bottom through the country of the Pottawatamies, until we came to McMeaken's trading post—here we were met by a half-breed messenger from Bulboni's, on horseback. He rode up to the wagon in which our two guides were, and after speaking but a few words, one of the Indians got out of the wagon and mounted the horse on which the messenger had come, and having turned his head, rode directly back the way which we had come. I was very much surprised at the alacrity with which he went on some errand away back several miles, for he had to go several miles to get *anywhere!* This was singular, when one considers that these Indians had been travelling at least five days, and camping out five nights! But there is nothing like getting used to it. The messenger jumped into the wagon, and on we went. In an hour or so we were at Bulboni's. The house is situated about a half mile from the bank of the Kansas. It is a large log house, built in the form of a cross. When we had entered, we discovered that it looked as if it had once been used for a Roman Catholic Church; but we think not. There were three rooms, or apartments. The arms of the cross, as it were, were partitioned off from the main apartment. To speak

4*

ecclesiastico-architecturally, the transepts were railed off from the nave. These transepts formed chambers, and the nave was used for "everything in particular." Bulboni had been a nabob among the Pottawatamies, but he was now dead. The inmates of the house now consisted of the widow Bulboni, two grown-up male Bulbonis, and two full-grown female Bulbonis, a young Miss Bulboni, and a being which I must turn over to Agassiz,—it had female clothes on—it had *red, curly* hair, negro nose and lips, Indian high cheek bones, and a complexion of the mulatto order. If it must have a name and a habitation, why let us try it,—Africo-Indo-Franko-Americano-Pottawattamie! If the naturalists wish an abbreviation, why, they may send for it, and put it in the Museum! I have described the animal for them, and I have no doubt but that it is in the same woods still; they use it at Bulboni's in the capacity of a slave, and of course it is *for sale,* no matter *whose* blood, or of what nation, courses through its veins! Did I not say well, that Mr. Pickwick would have had "hoccupation" on this journey?

The Bulbonis could talk English, but they would not. So we had to converse by our interpreter. The Doctor had to gather an account of all the symptoms of the sick girl, through this channel. How absurd! The Miss Bulboni was sitting some distance from her sister; the doctor asked the being above described, *when* Miss Bulboni was going to be *married?* They all burst out a laughing—this was an *interesting* point.

"Now," said the Doctor, "I wish you to talk English to me; this, your daughter, and your sister, cannot live long, unless there is something done for her very soon."

They were all endowed with the gift of the English tongue as if by miracle. The Doctor left very lengthy directions, and told the young men to come into Weston in a week, or ten days, and tell him how she then might be. We remained all night at Bulboni's. We left for home quite early the next morning. I will here state that the girl lingered for a month longer, and then died.

On the first day's travel towards home, we made Charley Hart's, at Hickory Point. Charley was, and is, a character. Charley had, with much forethought, located himself at Hickory Point. If a carriage should start from Kickapoo, Leavenworth City, or Fort Leavenworth, the probabilities would be, that it would reach Charley's just about supper-time; and Charley, who was a Boniface of the good old stamp, would undoubtedly step out and open the carriage-door, order the trunks off, and the horses driven round, not *now* to the *barn*, but to the *place where* the barn is to be. But, if a train of wagons should be started from Fort Leavenworth, heavily laden, going into the interior, why, then, Charley would be out and give them a welcome on the *second* evening. The first night, they would have stopped at Dawson's. Dr. Bonnifant now introduced me to Charley. I had heard of Charley at Weston, when he lived there; but, he not being in *society*, I never had the honor of his acquaintance. My conscience smote me for not having sought Charley out; for he now confessed that he was early educated in the

Episcopal Church—he hoped that I would come out about Christmas, and preach for *them!* I asked him who "them" were? "Oh," said Charley, "we are always full, here." "Ha, ha, Charley, you wish me to come out fifty miles to preach, and fetch my congregation along with me." Charley shook his sides, and jocularly inquired if I was not from "away down East?" I replied, that "New Yorkers" never acknowledged to the name "*Yankee.*" I was obliged to be very cautious, lest an exciting discussion should be started on "gooseology." The name, "Yankee," generally took the spigot out of the barrel, and blood would often flow. I am rather of a spare habit. I never had to endure depletion. I had contracted a habit of sparing my remarks on the "goose," lest they should bleed me without taking a nice estimate of the weight or measure. I have often passed muster by sneering at a Yankee, just as I used heartily to do when a boy in New York. Perhaps some of my readers may not be aware that, in Missouri, they call all *Northern* men, Yankees; while the New Yorkers class only those who are from the New England States, as Yankees. You will at once, therefore, perceive how I could preserve both my conscience and my head, by sneering *occasionally* at the mention of the term. The company which I would be in then, *would* conclude (*I* could not help it) that I was sound on the "goose," and they would give me the "liberty of the city," whether the city was built, or only in *contemplation,* as was generally the case in Kansas.

But let us get into Charley's hospitable log-cabin.

He began making apologies from the moment that we started for the door. He had concluded that I was not a "stingy Yankee," and would, therefore, expect him to have a good fire and a good supper. When we had got into the little seven-by-nine reception room, there was a stove about the size of a "Pearl-Starch Box," with a pipe made out of the odds and ends of all pipes; there was a length of four-inch pipe, new—this fitted the stove; then, the next length was old, and a five-inch pipe; the next was old, too, and a six-inch pipe; these were kept from collapsing by cloths stuffed in tightly where the joints came together; otherwise they would all have shut up together, like the different lengths in a spy-glass, when it has been well worn. The stove itself was set up on two tiers of bricks, so as to elevate the whole sufficiently to permit the last length of the pipe to go up through a hole cut in the side of the roof, designed hereafter to allow of a chimney. The whole contrivance had evidently been extemporised for our benefit; therefore, Charley deserved nothing but blessing. I don't know how the Doctor felt—he said nothing; but my own feelings were all in Charley's favor.

I saw that Charley had set his heart upon having Hickory Point made a city. He took me out to show me a discovery which he had made, and pointed to a stratum of slate, which indicated coal formation. He pointed out further a beautiful knoll, on which a church would look quite picturesque. This he would be generous enough to give for such a purpose! Charley would have me believe that his heart was in the right place,

by this display of generosity. Poor Charley thought
that I was as simple as I looked; he did not for a moment think that I was aware that I might put a church
on every hill-top for fifty miles round, if I had the
means merely to get the logs drawn. He professed,
more and more, his sincere love for "my Church" (he
had *forgotten* the word Episcopal).

When I got back to Weston, I told the people of
Charley's generosity. I there learned that whenever
Charley went anywhere to meeting, it was to the
Campbellite Baptist; still, for the encouragement of
any enthusiastic missionary, I will say that, if he will
go and establish a church there, build it himself, board
and clothe himself, and preach every Sunday, there is
every hope that Charley will be a *follower*—he will
commit himself to your course of policy and way of
thinking, from the very first day; perhaps you had
better wait until he proposes a place on his claim for
the church; if you are too eager to go there, he may
charge you a trifle for the land. Have a little worldly
wisdom; like Jacob Faithful, "keep cool."

After supper, which was decidedly the most inviting
meal which had been set before us since we left Weston, Charley, the Doctor, and one or two others, together with myself, returned to the seven-by-nine
reception room. Here Charley entertained us by a
relation of incidents connected with the battles in
Mexico, under Taylor. Charley had been the "General's *orderly.*" They say that no man is a hero in the
estimation of his *valet de chambre*—but I must say that
Old Rough and Ready could bear close inspection, if

Charley Hart can be trusted. Palo Alto and Resaca de la Palma were mono-dramaticized, to my infinite amusement, in that little seven-by-nine reception room, at Hickory Point, K. T. Charley—

"Shoulder'd his crutch, and show'd how fields were won."

Charley said that he would go outside and show it off; but there being no high hills to represent "Palo Alto," he could do just as well in the cabin. We told Charley not to go out into the cold; that we would rather stretch our imaginations inside of the cabin, than our limbs outside, particularly as it was dark; and we would have to follow him closely, to be able to gain any idea of the action of that famous battle! There was one point in Charley's narrative which I am well satisfied belongs to the secret history of those stirring times. He told us that General La Vega, I think this was the name, I cannot lay my hand on the *documents*, was captured and disarmed by a private in the American army,—that the private was rewarded by being placed under *arrest* for his bravery! Charley concluded, "that as long as such was the rule of the *service*, that humble men had better seek glory in the volunteer ranks, under such men as Doniphan." He believed that it was a natural instinct, confined to no condition, that when the rewards and promotions were about to be made, for every man to come forward and claim his due. As, for instance, when the Duke of Wellington, after one of his great victories, was bestowing promotions with no sparing hand, the *servant* of

Charles O'Malley, Mickey Free, put in his claim. "Ah, Masther Charley, if it was but a gauger."

It had now got to be nine o'clock, in Charley Hart's cabin. I observed an interesting glance or two pass between Charley and the Doctor. I did not at once understand what it meant. But after a few minutes, Charley came and whispered to me. "We have but few comforts here *yet* in the line of beds and bedding." "Now," continued he, "I want you to be made as comfortable as *possible*, before any of the others go to bed." I took the hint at once, and retired with Charley. He showed me into another room in the log, ten-by-twelve, perhaps. I prepared to retire, while Charley stood over me talking in a very pious strain. I got into the bed, and Charley laid seven or eight heavy blankets over me, and tucked them in round the edges. "This," he observed, "was necessary;" saying, "It is going to be a cold night," and pointed to the many unchinked holes around the room. I thanked him very much for his kindness, when he retired. I heard a chuckle in the other room, when Charley re-entered it. In about fifteen minutes afterward I heard a queer noise in the seven-by-nine   "Click," "click," "click," "click," "click," "click," "click." "Thump," "thump," (loud,) "thump," (louder,) "thump," (loudest,) and "ha! ha! ha!" "Chink," "chink," "chink," went the halves and quarters, making change! Charley's anxiety for my comfort in bed was explained! He remembered the Doctor's penchant for card-playing at Weston, and he thought that he would play a game in diplomacy with me. I was wheedled into *retirement!*

I think that if President Pierce had had Charley at his elbow when he had the removal of Reeder under consideration, he would have succeeded much more smoothly! However this might have been, I was reminded forcibly of the truth that "the children of this world are, in their generation, wiser than the children of light."

I had got to sleep, when I was awakened by what I supposed to be the sound of many waters, dripping in through the roof. I listened for a moment and then opened mine eyes. I observed a light in the room. I shifted in the bed, and the gurgling sound ceased at once! Charley softly made for the door, with a tin measure of about a quart in size, in his hand; and the odor which he left behind him was as if it had been "Bourbon," such as Davy Atchison would have relished! I got to sleep again, and slept until morning. When I rose to dress myself, I lifted a cloth, which hung gracefully over a barrel in the corner of the room, and I discovered, marked on the end of the barrel, "Rectified Whiskey." The mysteries of the night were opened.

Every time that I passed Charley, in the morning until the moment of departure, he was just as piously inclined as he had been on the night previous. He was ignorant altogether of my discoveries.

CHAPTER XVI.

CHARLEY HART GETS THE UNANIMOUS VOTE OF HIS
DISTRICT AS A CANDIDATE FOR THE LEGISLATURE,
YET FAILS OF AN ELECTION.

AFTER what I have said of Charley in a former
chapter, the reader will at once perceive that he had
every requisite to gain popularity. One word with
reference to the district itself. Charley's log was the
only house within twenty miles, in any direction;
consequently Charley was popular, he had no competitors. My visit to Charley's was made some months
before the election, it is true; but the severe winter intervened, and therefore we may well judge that no
great settlement had been made so far in the interior
during that season. I must draw upon my knowledge
of the previous circumstances to justify my remarks in
this chapter. The place of holding the election had been
appointed by Governor Reeder at Charley's house, because he could not have appointed it elsewhere! There
were four or five white men staying at Charley's when
I was there; one or two of these were serfs, Charley
being the feudal lord of the domain. A convention
to put a man in nomination for the Legislature was of
course called by the hangers-on of Charley, *i. e.*, the
hangers-on addressed themselves, and said: "Let us
meet in mass convention and nominate a man faithful

and true to *our interests*, to represent us in the Legislative Halls of our Territory."

Five persons attended this mass meeting. Charley Hart, Esq., was called to the Chair. On motion, the appointment of Secretary was sought to be dispensed with, lest there should be no speakers! This motion was decided out of order by the Chairman. He said · " That a day might come when a record of that day's proceedings would be sought for as historical data. I may be mistaken, gentlemen," continued he, " but my hopes are sanguine, that we are standing on ground hereafter to become the seat of a mighty empire! It is true that this is an interior point, but railroads, I heard a fellow once say, would have the tendency to build up cities in the interior of a country, as in former times caravans had done.

" He said a great deal about Egypt and Asia Minor, and such countries, and I became a convert to his opinion. I think that Hickory Point is to have a glorious future; and since you have done me the honor to appoint me the Chairman of the first meeting of a public character, I would like to have a record kept of the proceedings. The name of Charley Hart, in such a case, would go down to posterity with honor."

Here Charley showed symptoms of tears. The gentleman who made the motion withdrew it: " He expressed the hope that he would not be appointed Secretary—he had *private* reasons why he did not wish the honor."

The rest of the gentlemen present also declined being Secretary.

"Gentlemen," said Charley, "I think I can guess why you all decline this honor. Jerry," said Charley, "just go into the kitchen and ask Aunt Esther to come out here; she is a 'free nigger,' and was taught to write a little by an Abolition preacher over in Weston; we can make use of her, while one of you can have his name signed to the proceedings."

The gentlemen said, "that the suggestion of their worthy Chairman was a good one, but hoped that Aunt Esther would be made to sit outside of the room by the window, as they could not place themselves on a level with negroes."

There was no objection to this arrangement. Aunt Esther was called, and told to go outside the window, and act as Secretary to the meeeting.

"Act as what?" said Aunt Esther.

The more intelligent ones laughed at this question.

"I'll show you," said Charley. He went now in search of a sheet of paper, which had been forgotten, and returned with what appeared to be a fly-leaf taken out of some book which he had in his trunk. Pen and ink were now inquired for. Aunt Esther had to go and get her's. She returned, and was told "that what they wanted her to do was to set down whatever they should say or do." "In the first place," said Charley, "set down, that at a meeting of the Squatter Sovereigns of Hickory Point, K. T., held on,—Jerry, what day of the month is this?"

Jerry did not know, "he had not kept any count." They all tried now to recall circumstance after circum-stance, likely to fix the day of the month, but in vain.

"Well," said Charley, "never mind, there will be a train out from the Fort to day or to-morrow, I have no doubt, then we shall learn." " Held on ————, Charles Hart, Esq., was appointed Chairman, and Jerry Walker, Secretary."

Here Aunt Esther said that "she thought that she had been appointed *that!*"

" No," said Charley, "you merely do the writing."

The meeting now being duly organized, the Chairman stated the object of it, which was "to place in nomination a candidate for the Legislature." The circular from the Governor was here read, which marked out the boundaries of the districts, and the places of holding the election in each. Charles Hart, Esq., Chairman, went on to say, that "great discretion was to be used in selecting a candidate for so important a post; he hoped that their *own* interests and the interest of Hickory Point would be the only considerations which would be allowed to weigh with them."

Timothy Spooner obtained the floor after the Chairman had taken his seat. Tim went on to say, "For my part, my own good, and the good of Hickory Point, I go for the election of Char*less* Hart, Esquire." (Great cheering, in which Aunt Esther joined.)

The Chairman here rose to correct the Hon. gentleman: " The election was not now being held, that it was a nomination, as they call it; that is to say, putting a person forward to be elected when the time comes."

" Well," said Tim, " that is what I mean.)

The Chairman went on to remark further, "that from

present appearances, the nomination of a candidate will be just the same as an election."

"Very well, then," remarked Tim, "I don't see where I was wrong."

"In order to make the thing right," said the Chairman, "it will be necessary that the motion of the honorable gentleman, Timothy Spooner, be seconded."

Jerry here spoke, and said, "that if there was anything wanting that he could do, he would do it; but he would like to know who was going to have charge of the house while Charley was gone to the Legislature."

Charley's sagacity here suggested to him that the discussion of this question would be the springing of a mine that would blow his ambitious aspirations sky-high, if he were not exceedingly careful.

"Does the honorable gentleman insist upon an answer to his question to-day?" said the Chairman.

"If the nomination is just the same as an election," said Jerry, "I do."

"Then," said the Chairman, "I intend that while I am gone to the Legislature, you shall all take care of each other, and the house shall be at your service!" (Great cheering.)

Jerry now said, "then just make the thing to suit yourselves."

The Chairman rose to put the question. "It is moved by the Honorable Timothy Spooner, and seconded by Jerry—Jerry what is your other name, I have forgotten it?"

"Walker," said Jerry.

"And seconded by Jerry Walker, that Charles Hart, Esq., be, and hereby is, the unanimous choice of the Squatter Sovereigns of Hickory Point to represent them in the Legislature of Kansas. All those in favor of this motion say aye,"—this sign was given unanimously.

Aunt Esther here remarked, "that she could not take it down just as it was said."

This observation has been made by more than one Secretary before Aunt Esther; it shows the importance of putting resolutions in *writing*.

The Chairman said "that he would attend to the wording of the resolution afterwards." He rose now to return thanks for the unexpected honor which had been conferred upon him: "Gentlemen, I thank you from the bottom of my heart. I am well satisfied that if the district were more thickly settled, that you would have had a larger number to choose from, but I think that you would not have found one more disposed to carry out measures which will be for your interest. I regard my election as certain; therefore I will here state what I think will be much to our interest. The alteration of the Delaware Treaty is of the first importance; it is true that Tom Benton says, 'that we are here on the Military *outlet*;' but perhaps you may know, as well as I do, that old General Jackson is no more, and that Col. Benton is now left nowhere. It may be that the Legislature will appoint a Committee to go to Washington to see about the alteration of this treaty, and if such should be the will of that Honorable body, I think that I will stand a good chance of being selected, in consequence of my personal acquaintance with General Pierce in Mexico."

Timothy Spooner said, " that their interests were safe in the hands of their chosen standard-bearer !"

Aunt Esther was here told to go and put on the kettle for the whiskey punches.

We can well imagine how slowly the weeks passed which intervened between the time of this important event in the history of the feudal lord of Hickory Point, and the day of election; they must have appeared months at least, in the calendar of Charley Hart. But his anxiety was, after all, the blissful dream. It is only the pursuit of an object which seems to please.

Charley Hart had been on the field of battle; he had conversed with Generals of division, and Generals in chief command, as a man talketh with his neighbor; but yet all this did not satisfy his ambition—another theatre now appeared to present itself:

> " Let arms revere the robe,
> The warrior's laurel yield
> To the palm of Eloquence."

Bright was the future for mine host of Hickory Point; all things glittered, and everything which glittered was gold. Jerry Walker and Timothy Spooner, several times before the day of election, took instalments on the promise which Charley had given, namely, ' that while he was gone they should take care of each other, and the house should be at their service." It is true that they gave too loose a construction to this promise; Charley had said, " that the good time of guardianship to each other, and the freedom of appropriating the good things which might be at the Hickory Point Head inn to themselves without money and without price, and without work, would come *when* he had departed for the attendance on the Legislature at Pawnee;" but he was too shrewd a man not to perceive the imminent hazard in which he would place his affairs if he should insist on a "strict construction"—he wisely, therefore, resolved to stoop to conquer.

Jerry, often, with perfect nonchalance, took down the box of the best cigars which the cabin afforded, and helped himself and his particular friend Tim; not infrequently would Tim pay a friendly visit to the barrel of "Rectified." Such services as these they were as much too ready to perform, as they were remiss to give the welcome to the stranger, for whose sake Charley had exiled himself to Hickory Point. The reputation of the house suffered severely during the month previous to the election; it may be that the disaster extended itself, and had its effect in the final result. Aunt Esther was the only one who remained faithful to the interest and service of her master; though she was free, she did not abuse her freedom. Charley may have thanked that "Common Law" of the Anglo-Saxon race—indeed, we may say, of the race of Adam (with the exception of a few Bloomers)—which does not permit the right of suffrage to a woman, less a *black* woman, much less a *free* black woman!—the masters take the liberty to vote for the *interests* (?) of the *slave* black woman, in some parts of our consistent confederacy; but our Blackstone, when he comes to set forth

the rights of man, must make some exceptions in behalf of model Republicans!   Charley Hart was grate-
ful to the genius of our institutions, that Aunt Esther
enjoyed not the elective franchise; for, had she possessed
this boon, she might have become as useless as those
who would not allow themselves to be placed on a level
with free negroes; and the efforts of the master of Hickory Point, in behalf of the travelling public, would have
become paralyzed.   But, of course, the candidate for
the highest office in the gift of the "squatter sovereigns"
of Hickory Point, was too good a politician to permit
his brow to wrinkle, his eye to glance wrath, his tongue
to speak reproach, his hand to administer cuffs, or his
foot to give *stern* rebukes.   In truth, Charley's constituency was a "free constituency."   It is a remarkable fact that the nearer we descend to the common
level among men, the better do we get to realize the
true import of phrases.   "The people" from whom we
spring, call things by their right names, and enjoy the
things to which the right names are given. It was well
known to those hangers-on of Charley's, that power
emanated from the people.   They also knew, however
much they pretended ignorance, "that nomination for
office was *not* the same as election thereto;" but a small
portion of the power, therefore, had as yet departed
from them, and they fully determined that indemnifi-
cation should take place ere they they should be shorn,
and, like Samson, become as other men.   They made
a loud cry for the "collaterals," in the shape of cigars,
whiskey, freedom from chopping fire-wood, driving
home the cows, and milking them.   Charley's strength

was to sit still, and quietly submit to his masters. But compensation is the law of nature, and to this law Charley now submitted himself; and what he could not withhold, in the form of cigars and whiskey, without bringing ruin in its train, he determined, like many others, to make a virtue of necessity, and " gave himself the *pleasure*" to present the cigars and whiskey, as frequently as the recipients thought they were needful!

The day for the election was now near. Prairie chickens and partridges were procured for the dinner; a luxury which they had often enjoyed before—but no rarer could be obtained.

On the day previous to the election, towards evening, a company of fifty or sixty men on horseback, having each shot guns, or other arms, camped near Hickory Point. The proprietor of the Point fancied that they were a party of hunters, on an expedition. There was nothing about their appearance which indicated that they were immigrants; they had no wagons with farming utensils, no oxen or cows. Charley's mind was set at rest. " They would all leave in the morning." Morning came, and there was promise of a quiet election day. The strangers did not seem to be making any preparations for leaving, as hunters might be expected to do. Mine host went out to greet them. He discovered that the good report of Hickory Point had travelled further than he could have hoped for—the party *was* an immigrant party! looking out for a location ; and they were more than pleased with Hickory Point ! " They were determined to locate there, and, on the morrow, the great majority of them would return, for their wives and children, and stock. Understanding that the election was to be held there that day, they had come out, to give a direction to the future destinies of Hickory Point and Kansas Territory." Charley Hart was amazed. It was a most singular turn which now seemed to present itself in his affairs. If they were true men, of course they would respect his claims, and, particularly, the nomination made by the squatters, in mass convention, at Hickory Point. That things might be brought to a happy conclusion, he thought that a little *spiritual* influence should be used; he invited the party up to the "log," to taste his "Bourbon." It was acknowledged, with many an oath, to be the genuine article. The merits of St. Louis, Cincinnati, and Bourbon County, Kentucky, whiskey, were discussed, *con amore*—and the more they tasted of that quality which they enjoyed on the present occasion, the more animated they became, in the praises of those "brands" which they did not possess. One of them here ventured to remark, with a tremendous oath, that "he supposed that those —— Yankees would be for introducing a 'Maine Law' into the Legislature." Charley here remarked, "that, on this head, he would use his influence against that most unconstitutional law, in the halls of the Legislature. Several here inquired, if Charley "expected to go to the Legislature?" He replied, that he had been expecting nothing else for the last month, and that the affairs of his house had been conducted exclusively on such a supposition! He ventured to hope "that, if they were about to cast their lot in with them at Hickory Point, that their vote would help to place him in a position for which he thought himself in some degree qualified." It was answered to this, that "Mr. Hart was a stranger to them, and, as the general practice was for the majority to decide, it would have to be submitted to that issue!" The blood of Charley's system fled to his heart, for refuge.

There was now but one way in which this election could be decided in his favor, and that was by a rigid administration of the oath provided by Gov. Reeder, to qualify for exercising the franchise in doubtful cases.

"Of course," said Charley, "gentlemen, you will have no objection to take the oath prescribed by the Governor?"

"Not in the least—did it accord with their principles; but, in their case, it would interfere with their privilege —they were Quakers!"

"Why," said Charley, "I thought that the Quakers swore not at all?"

"O, bless you, the Hicksites can swear on all occasions, except useful ones—we are Hicksites!"

They stood on their "privileged question," and Charley, though he got all the legal votes in his district, yet failed of an election!

CHAPTER XVII.

A MACEDONIAN CRY WHEN LIBERALLY CONSTRUED.

MY readers, I hope, will bear in mind that our pioneer Clergy are not as numerous as those of the different denominations in the country. The laity, who are scattered abroad in the different parts of our new settlements, repeatedly deplore their want of privileges which are enjoyed by their "more favored brethren." The sight of an Episcopal clergyman is regarded by them as a harbinger of the advance of civilization, as decided as the flight of the birds to the northward, is an indication of the return of Spring.

When I left father and mother, and an Eastern home, and rejected proffered parishes in the most pleasant, and in Summer, the most *fashionable*, of neighborhoods, to take an invalid wife, and a sweet child, whose eyes were to be closed in death on the journey, and go to preach the Gospel of the grace of God to the people on the extreme border of civilization, then I felt that I had every reason to say, in some measure, at least, with the Apostle, "And I know that when I come unto you, I shall come in the *fulness* of the blessing of the Gospel of Christ."

I had reason to hope that a communicant, who had two brothers in the Ministry of the Church—that another communicant, to whom I had first administered the sacred emblems of the broken body and the shed blood of the Son of God, would receive me, comfort me, and hold up my feeble hands, while God made me the humble instrument to bring salvation to the many whom they knew to be there "in the gall of bitterness and in the bonds of iniquity !" If there had been other communicants in that my field of labor, " Fort Leavenworth and parts adjacent," with whom I had had the slightest acquaintance, then I would not have felt so much discouraged ; but there was not a male communicant save these two in all my field of labor, *to my knowledge.*

But I did not only suffer neglect from these gentlemen ; I was secretly and openly opposed by them ; my good efforts were thwarted ; the advances which I had made towards the completion of cherished plans for " Church extension," were suddenly stayed by these emissaries, whom I cannot call " of God."

One of these communicants called me into his office, one day, in Weston, Mo. Said he to me, ' I am now about removing into the Territory, and I would like to know what course you are about to pursue in the contest which we know must come ?" This was an astounding question. It suggested everything which I could wish to have said in my favor ! It most conclusively proved *that he had never heard me in any speech or discourse indicate which course I was about to pursue in the affairs of the Territory !* Oh, fortunate and unfortunate question ! Fortunate for me, unfortunate for my enemies. Come, gentlemen, I challenge you for the proof that I ever made a speech or ever delivered a discourse against the institution of Slavery! Mark me, I do not make this challenge as an apology to you or to others. I give not up one tittle of my *private* hatred of the Institution—neither do I promise that from henceforth I shall be as silent as I have been in times gone by—no, mine enemies, you have by your persecutions and by your shedding of innocent blood, imbued my heart with as intense a hatred of Slavery as ever Hannibal felt towards the Romans!

But I must answer the question of my worthy communicant. Said I, " Sir, my influence, in a becoming manner, shall be used to make Kansas a Free State. I am to reside therein. I love Freedom, and Free Institutions." "Well," said he, "I think that you ought to be altogether passive in the matter." He quoted a text: " Render unto Cæsar the things which are Cæsar's, and unto God the things which are God's." I gave him, in reply, a very summary interpretation of the text. Said I, " If I shall be fortunate enough to acquire any property over in Kansas, I trust that I shall be able and willing to pay my taxes." The gentleman rose, and the audience was over.

The other communicant was an officer in the Army of the United States. He was interested in Leavenworth City, a point which I considered within my mission, but for a reason to be noted, I did not make anxious efforts to obtain a site for a church.* The United States Army officer was asked, as I am informed by the petitioner himself, for a contribution towards the erection of a house of worship for a re

* This property belongs to the Delaware Indians.

spectable denomination of Christians, at Leavenworth City. The officer declined, and gave his reasons, which were, "that the Episcopal church would make as large demands upon him as he could well meet." "It was then in contemplation to erect an Episcopal church at Leavenworth City. That he had offered two lots in the city to the 'Domestic Committee' in New York, with the promise also of five hundred dollars more, provided the Committee would furnish fifteen hundred dollars." "Is Mr. ——" (naming the writer) "to be the Minister?" "No, sir," in the most decided manner, answered the army officer.

I repeated these facts to the Rev. Mr. Irish, of St. Joseph. Mr. I. acknowledged to me that such were the plans! I made complaint to my Bishop at once. I have good reasons to believe that my Bishop represented my complaint to the proper quarter, but of this I cannot be sure; at any rate, the Rev. Mr. Irish was instructed by *his* Bishop to confine his labors and interest solely to his own field of labor in Missouri. I have the best of authority for this, the declaration of Mr. I. himself, and the notoriety of the circumstance at St. Joseph, Missouri.

Now I continued to officiate at Kickapoo, neither of my male communicants ever attended service there; I officiated at Leavenworth, neither of them attended there. I asked a lawyer, who now resided in Leavenworth, but who had once been a vestryman of mine in Weston, if he would not let me have his Law office to officiate in? "He dare not do so!" He talked for the "goose," but I could read him pretty well. I *knew* that he was not *sound* on the animal; and my prognostications have proved correct; he has since been elected by the Free State party Attorney-General? The subscription for a church at Kickapoo was abandoned. I wonder if there had been any tampering in that quarter? I am *sure* of it!

Where did these " High churchmen " attend service on Sunday? Did they have a chaplain of the Episcopal church at Fort Leavenworth? No, thank God, the church has been saved that disgrace! My blood boiled within my veins, when I saw it once published in a Chicago journal, that the chaplain at Fort Leavenworth belonged to the Episcopal church. It is not true. Reader, what would you think of it, if I were to tell you that I was the only clergyman of the Episcopal church in Kansas Territory, save the chaplain at Fort Riley, an honor to his profession, and that these, my communicants, never attended my services—never attended the services of him whom they believed was alone ordained of God, as was Aaron, to minister in Holy things? Would you not say that "the come over and help us " of these gentlemen and others, was " A Macedonian cry when *liberally* construed?"

CHAPTER XVIII.

LAW AND GOSPEL; A VICE-PRESIDENT PREACHES A CRUSADE, AND AN OLD SCHOOL CHAPLAIN SELLS IN-DULGENCES.

I PRESUME that there is hardly a people in any section of our country, neither is there any community on the face of the earth, which might not be incited to exercise violence toward a weaker party, if the instigators should be the second in power in the nation, and his recommendations approved by a minister of the "Religion of Love!" provided the arguments which were used would go to show, that if the majority did not exercise this violence, their homes and their institutions would be laid prostrate in the dust! If such a course would be pursued, I say, in our most staid, and enlightened, and law-loving sections of our country, might we not reckon upon such a result with unerring certainty among the communities on our border?

A gentleman, occupying for many years the very high honor of representing in part, his entire State in the Senate of a great Republic, and there by a great majority of his fellow-senators from the different States, chosen to preside over their most important legislative debates, to sign the most important acts in the legislation of a great and free people, and thereby, *ex officio*, the second personage in the Republic, by and with whose advice, together with the body over which he presided, the Executive of the nation could neither turn to the right hand or to the left, takes the high responsibility of inflaming the minds and passions of a highly-excitable body of people in his own State, and in his own county, to go, in open defiance of all law, and of all justice, and in opposition to the instincts of humanity, fallen and low as these are, into a neighboring Territory, and there abuse, and drive out, and if need be, destroy a people, the descendants emphatically of those who bled and died in securing the liberties of our country. Can we be at all astonished that the people thus urged did not stop short of bloodshed? I state without the least fear of positive and convincing contradiction, that such was the drift of speeches delivered by the person above alluded to, and published, not in full, or from manuscript furnished, but from reporters' notes, in the "Platte Argus," published at Weston, Mo.

Why should a man question his obvious duty, when advised by such an oracle? What remained to be done but armed organization? And this was effected in all the counties of North-Western Mo., tó my personal knowledge. Stronger language was never used in the days of the Revolution, by the orators, when they incited rebellion against an odious tyranny, distant nearly four thousand miles from our shores, than was used by the servants of this Republic, and residents of a foreign State, to incite its inhabitants to bloodshed, and to the butchery of those who disagreed with them on a question, which has been nothing but a subject of dispute since the colonization of our country! And if we add to all this, that one calling himself a minister of the Prince of Peace, and one employed by the Executive of the nation, and whose services in such work are paid by the hard earnings of our people, came forward, in person, by speech-making, by pamphlet-printing, by doggerel verse-writing, and by Scripture-quoting, and these passages of Scripture sent to that vile sheet, the "Platte Argus," and there printed, with a challenge for refutation prefixed, why then bloodshed as advised by lawyers, became piety when advised by divines! There was indulgence in "High Heaven" for such enormous iniquities! The Court of Papal Rome, in her worst days, has been outdone by our Government, and a greater than Tetzel will be found among United States Chaplains, even in the middle of the nineteenth century! I did wonder whether the "Congressional Committee" would discover this pious parson; I rejoice that they did. I hope that they had it proved, for it was very susceptible of proof, that this parson printed a pamphlet in favor of Slavery, attended a meeting of the famous "Self-Defensives," at Platte City, and there delivered a doggerel verse poem burlesqueing philanthropy, which was afterwards published in the "Platte Argus," and the mildest term which I can give of the drift of all was, "that the Free State settlers in Kansas Territory must be *got rid of!*"

This pious soul is yet allowed to preach the Gospel, and to set a good example to the officers and soldiers at one of our military posts, in Kansas Territory, and to communicants of my own Church, who, if they had but said the word, might have enjoyed an occasional service from me, a minister whom they had every confidence in, until they learned I was not in favor of Slavery extension, and particularly opposed to the extension of that institution into Territory which had been consecrated to Freedom, and in which I had hoped to do much good.

These are facts. A Vice-President preached a crusade for the recovery from Freedom of a Territory of immense extent, to be devoted, when wrested from the hands of lawful settlers, to Slavery forever; and to the crusaders who should enrol themselves for this work a hope of gaining heaven was afforded, according to the construction of the act by common minds, and promise of Indulgence was given!

The texts of Scripture which the parson had printed, and a challenge for refutation prefixed to them, I at once acknowledge, recognize the existence of a kind of bondage; but it was such a bondage as permitted an Apostle to commend a slave to his Master as a *brother in Christ;* such a bondage as allowed of the attainment of the very highest knowledge of letters, as for instance, the example of the poet Terence; it was such a bondage as permitted the bondman to become the intimate friend and companion of his Master, and of his Master's friends. The mere recognition of the existence of an institution on the part of the Inspired writers is no guarantee that it was the design of the Almighty that such institutions should remain forever.

A remarkable case in point, is that where our Lord tells his disciples—" The Scribes and Pharisees sit in Moses' seat, whatsoever, therefore, they bid you observe, that observe and do." Where were the Scribes and Pharisees, and where was their seat of authority, forty years after this time?

It is nothing short of blasphemy to say that the Book of God will in its spirit recognize, and give authority to perpetuate, the Institution of African Slavery in America! I place in opposition, therefore, to Parson K.'s texts, the whole spirit of Christianity. His texts will recognize in those days the existence of a bondage such as I have above briefly described, and he will find texts which enjoin obedience to masters; but will he find the evils *inseparable* from a state of Slavery such as exists in the United States, in accordance with the Spirit of Christianity?

The Spirit of Christianity is at work—the Sun of Righteousness will melt away all the elements and remnants of barbarism, among which I class Slavery. This will be effected gradually, and in God's own good time. The social, moral, and political globe is gradually approaching its summer solstice. As surely as the frozen ice and snow are melted when old Terra gradually turns on its axis, and rolls on its orbit round the Sun, so will the remnants of barbarism disappear when the Sun of Righteousness shall have His *designed* influence!

CHAPTER XIX.

ESTIMATE OF GOVERNOR REEDER—"LARGE STREAMS FROM LITTLE FOUNTAINS FLOW."

IT is well known, I presume, in political circles that Governor Reeder gave his influence for the passage of the "Kansas Territorial Organization Bill"—in other words, he favored the repeal of the Missouri Compromise. In my opinion, the principle of this Bill would be right in its application, under some circumstances —as, for instance, should territory be acquired in the future by these States; but, in the case under consideration, I must be allowed to say that, in my opinion, it was wrong.

But I write not this work to give my opinions on political subjects like the above. I merely say these few words by way of introducing a character, not perfect, nor altogether consistent, but, in the main, highly honorable. Such an one was Gov. Reeder. He went into the Territory of Kansas with the full determination of carrying out, and with the strong persuasion of his ability to carry out the principles of the Kansas Bill. When he entered the Territory he was exceedingly cautious in his deportment, and altogether silent with regard to his own sentiments on the great question at issue. Free State men were very doubtful of his aid in their behalf. The Pro-Slavery party had no more assurance of his co-operation, than his approbation of the repeal of the Missouri Compromise gave them. They presumed on this sentiment of the Governor, and the leaders of the Pro-Slavery party—the "Weston Regency," the "Self-Defensive Club"—made great preparations to receive the Governor with much respect, by giving a public dinner in his honor, at the St. George Hotel, Weston, Mo. This was early in the fall of 1854. The Governor had just arrived in the Territory. The dinner was announced in the "Platte Argus." Expectation was on tip-toe. The card of invitation was published, and a courteous letter, declining the honor, by Gov. Reeder, was also published. From this day forth Gov. Reeder was branded as an Abolitionist, and said to be in league with the Emigrant-Aid Society. There never were more unfounded charges. Had they been true, Gov. Reeder would not have fallen in my estimation; but they were false. His acts, previous to any violation of law, were of a strictly impartial character; and his conduct after such infringement, was in vindication of law.

The Secretary of the Territory, a Pro-Slavery man, told me, "that he did not know what course Governor Reeder intended to pursue—that he never heard him declare his private opinion."

I desire now to state a few facts, in proof of what I have said. At Kickapoo City, in Kansas, where I officiated, at first, more frequently than at any other point, there was intense feeling on the vexed question. The occurrence which I am about to state took place a few weeks after the Governor first arrived in the Territory.

A petition for the appointment of a Justice of the Peace at Kickapoo, was prepared and taken to Gov. Reeder, then at the Shawnee Mission. The appointment was made by the Governor, without asking a question about the opinion of the person, whose appointment was asked for, on the subject of Slavery. The person appointed was a Free State man. This appointment gave great offence to the Pro-Slavery party in the town, and in Weston, Mo "The Kansas Pioneer," published at Kickapoo, had, in its next issue, a furious editorial, condemning the Governor, and calling a meeting to *elect* a Justice of the Peace. The people assembled, and elected E. S. Wilhite, a very respectable Pro-Slavery man. But this was done contrary to the Organic Law. Finally, a petition was prepared to the Governor, in behalf of Mr. Wilhite, asking his appointment to the office of Justice. The appointment was at once made by Gov. Reeder, while he, at the same time, remarked, " that he would appoint as many Justices as they thought they should need, whatever their politics might be."

This is a very fair specimen of the impartial course which Gov. Reeder endeavored to pursue, when he entered upon the execution of his duties.

The honor of Gov. Reeder has been called in question with reference to his pecuniary transactions. Of some of these transactions I cannot speak from any knowledge of the facts; but of that transaction which was made a pretext for his removal from office, I can speak. Governor Reeder and his party had passed a night at Charley Hart's, at Hickory Point, a day or two before my visit there, mentioned in a previous chapter. The terms of the contract with the Kaw half-breeds, which Gov. Reeder had made, were discussed in the little seven-by-nine reception room, at Charley's. The facts were gathered by Charley and others from Reeder and his party—it was my good fortune to learn the terms from those who were near neighbors of the half-breed Kaws. My informants were a gentleman by the name of Gray, son of a physician dwelling at Sparta, Mo., and another gentleman, whose name I do not recollect. These were residents near the mouth of Soldier Creek, a branch of the Kansas River, and very near neighbors to the Indians with whom Reeder had made the contract.

Charley Hart and his companions at Hickory Point had heard Gov. Reeder's statement—Mr. Gray and his friend had heard the Indians' statement of the transaction ;—notes were compared, in my presence and hearing, by both these parties, and they both agreed in this : " That the half-breed Kaws had, each, a section of land entailed, as it were, upon them for life, and to descend to their children ; but not subject to sale, without the consent of the President of the United States." Gov. Reeder made a contract with some three or four of these half-breeds for their lands, at the rate of " five dollars per acre, subject to the approbation of the President." Where is the over-reaching here ? and where is the dishonor ? The Indians, at that time, could not have obtained two dollars and a half per acre for their lands, from any other person than Gov. Reeder,—and the contract was made subject to the decision of the President.

This transaction was used against Reeder, in every paper published on the Border. My object, in mentioning these circumstances, is not the defence of Governor Reeder—he can defend himself; but I mention them to show the consistency of the policy pursued by the Pro-Slavery party, viz.: that no man was permitted to remain neutral. He who was not, heart and soul, in favor of Slavery extension, must be prepared to take extraordinary means to protect his honor and his life.

Soon after the occurrence of the fact above stated, the first election of Whitfield took place. I am well satisfied that he was elected by illegal votes. He was the Pro-Slavery candidate. I knew many in Missouri who said that they had voted for him. It was much feared that Gov. Reeder would not give a certificate to Whitfield. Many threats were made against his life, in the event of a refusal. But none of Whitfield's competitors contested his election before the Governor, and the certificate was furnished. Gov. Reeder must have been well satisfied of the enormous frauds practiced in this case, as I should judge, from his subsequent conduct.

He had the census taken during the winter, in the Territory. The returns showed a very large decrease in the number of those entitled to vote, compared with the number of those who had exercised the franchise when Whitfield ran the first time for Congress.

The Governor, after the returns were made, districted

the Territory, and issued a proclamation for the holding of the election for the members of the Territorial
Legislature. An oath was prescribed, to be administered
to the electors by the judges ; it infringed no right, but
if it had been allowed to be administered, I think it
would have effectually prevented the election of so
large a number of Pro-Slavery members. Gov. Reeder's subsequent conduct with the Legislature which was
said to be elected by the people of Kansas, is well known.
I will not dwell upon it.

The Governor's troubles began when he declined a
dinner, prepared for him at Weston, Mo., at which he
would have been called on to define his position. If
Weston had been in Kansas, perhaps he would have
gone—and perhaps he would not.

CHAPTER XX.

A SECRETARY OF STATE AND A PRIEST TALK POLITICS WITH THEIR NIGHT-CAPS ON.

ON account of my previous and more accurate knowledge of the topography of the eastern border of Kansas, I was often invited to take a stroll, by those who might have come from a distance to look at the country, and sometimes by the newly-appointed officers in the Territory.

On one of these rambles, in the neighborhood of Kickapoo Indian Village, in company with a clerk in one of the departments at Washington, a lawyer from Philadelphia, and Mr. Woodson from Virginia, the Secretary of the Territory, we got belated; and, as a place of refuge, where we might spend the night, I suggested the parsonage of the missionary among the Kickapoos. We accordingly went to this house, and were received very kindly.

The house was an old log structure, quite roomy for such a country. There were a few fruit trees about the house, and about twenty-five acres of land under cultivation. Various subjects suggested themselves for conversation during the evening.. The old missionary I have before alluded to—the Rev. N. T. Shaler, of the M. E. Church, South—suggested the " goose." It was utterly impossible to collect three or four persons to-

gether at any place, or in any house whatever, without the mention of the all-absorbing topic—Slavery.
The Rev. host commenced it this evening, by stating
that he was anxious to get a slave-servant for his wife.
I was well aware that this gentleman was sound on the
question, but I had hoped that we would be spared that
evening from listening to a lecture on the faith.

The old gentleman told us how sound the Rev. Mr.
Johnson, of his church, at the Shawnee Mission, was
on the "goose," and expressed the hope that that Reverend Brother would be put in nomination for Congress,
and elected! Here was one clergyman electioneer-
ing for a Reverend Brother, and the audience composed of a Clerk at Washington, a Philadelphia lawyer,
a Secretary of State, and an Episcopal clergyman. I
thought this was carrying the war into Africa without
any delicacy or fear as to the result. We had compared notes about the old man before we reached his
house, and had come to the conclusion that he was
very ignorant, but all allowed that his goodness would
balance his ignorance. The old gentleman did not
raise much of a breeze. For my own part, I saw that
it was an item of the bill to draw me out a *little further*
than I usually ventured. The old gentleman said that
he was going out forty miles further in the interior
with the Indians; that as he had pre-empted the claim
on which the old mission house stood, he would like to
sell his claim. I told him that I would purchase it,
and remove my wife from Weston at once to it. The
papers were drawn up, it was considered a bargain in
the house, and it soon got to be known on 'change.

But in about a week after this I was told that I could not have the place, as it had been promised to another person, which fact had escaped the old gentleman's recollection when he bargained with me! I was afterwards told in Weston that the "Directors" had tampered with the Parson, and persuaded him not to fulfil his engagement with me, as I was not sound on the "goose."

I was called on this evening to conduct evening prayer, but I declined; I would have been obliged to make an extemporaneous prayer, and I knew that anything extemporaneous from me would be dangerous. "A prayer for all sorts and conditions of men," contains the germs of Abolition!

The mistress of the house retired after worship, I do not know where. The Washington Clerk and the Lawyer from the City of Brotherly Love, were asked to make themselves comfortable together during the night; in like manner Secretary Woodson and myself were consigned to the same bed.

Secretary Woodson is a very handsome man, of about thirty years of age. He is quite tall and slender, very gentlemanly in manners and in conversation. He had been editor of the " Lynchburg (Virginia) Republican." He did not consider it his duty to be as reserved as was Governor Reeder, on the subject of Slavery in the Territory. He was in favor of its establishment. He did not appear to be fanatical on the subject. He discovered the same candor in me that I had found in him, although we differed in sentiment. We opened our minds to each other; I could not help liking the gentleman, and I think he must have taken a fancy to me, for he not only conversed on matters of public interest, but also on those which had concerned himself in the past.

He never anticipated, nor seemed to desire, that the people in Missouri should interfere to violate the ballot-box. He remarked, "that as far as he was concerned, justice should be done to both parties." I said, "that if the officers of the Territory would stand firm, and not allow certain gentlemen to control the affairs of the Territory, then I had every confidence that the final result would be as I desired." It did not appear to him that there was any important inter- est at stake, either of the North or of the South. He seemed to be a pro-slavery man from *taste*, and not on principle. He seemed to think that the Repeal of the Missouri Compromise was a Northern measure. I ac- knowledged that Northern politicians gave it their aid, but that no measure could be called Northern, unless the people of the North could take a warm interest in it, which it could not be said the Northern people had done. But I went on to say, that if Mr. Atchison and his friends in Missouri were to be credited, Mr. A. and a Senator from each of the States of Virginia and South Carolina, had used extraordinary persuasion with the Senator from Illinois, as Chairman of the Committee on Territories, to insert the repealing clause. I told him also, that Senator Atchison had made a speech in the Methodist Meeting-House, in Weston, two years ago, at which time he declared "that the Territory across the river, should not be organized, unless the people of Platte, and of Missouri, should have an opportunity of taking with them their Institutions, and settling there." That this declaration was in perfect consistency with a statement made to me by Colonel M., of St. Joseph, Mo., while we travelled together on board of one of the steamers on Lake Michigan, in the summer of 1854. Col. M. had spent the winter and spring at Washington, during which the "Kansas Bill" was pending. Col. M. told me that it was the general remark, "that a Senator from Missouri, and one from each of the States of Virginia and South Carolina, had more to do with the Committee on Territories, than the Committee-men did." He stated the circumstances much more pointedly and interestingly than this, but I do not feel justified in giving his exact words. Senator Atchison, since the passage of the Bill, made a speech in Kansas, in which he appropriated a considerable share of the glory attending the Repeal of the Missouri Compromise to himself. Senator Douglas, I believe, has never denied that there were interesting debates held on that measure, on occasions when a Quorum of the Senate was not present."

The Secretary "did not deny that all these statements were correct." I replied, that as far as my own statement was concerned, I knew that it was correct. Senator Atchison, at home, talks to the people in quite an interesting manner. He would never do for the head of the "Circumlocution Office." He gives valuable information of how he does things, and how things can be done.

If "you want to know, you know," why he can tell you. There are few who can speak with more *authority*.

The Secretary and myself placed ourselves several times during the night in a sleeping position; but the god of slumbers did not seem to interest himself in our behalf. We would turn over again, as some interesting point would present itself. There was no end to the momentous questions which the state of things presented.

The Secretary inquired about Church affairs at Kickapoo City. I was glad that he called my attention to these. I proceeded to talk on this subject, without the least interruption, for a long time. I repeated what I had hoped to do, and told him what little I had been able to accomplish.

I asked him what his opinion was on the statement which I had made. I received no answer. His nightcap had got down over his ears.

" Si vis me [dormire] flere dolendum est, primum ipsi tibi." If you wish me to sleep, then you had better go to sleep before me.

CHAPTER XXI.

A HIGH CHURCH PARSON TAKES LUTHER FOR A MODEL.

I SHOULD not be at all surprised to be asked, "how it happened that I did not meet with the fate which befell others as good and as true as myself?" Perhaps those who received the adornment of "tar and feathers" were *too* good! "Be not zealous over much," is the injunction of the Apostle.

Those who went up the Missouri to the Kansas Border in a "furor of Freedom," were simple enough to fancy that the ægis of the Constitution extended over, and protected the citizens of this Union, in the expression of their honest sentiments, in any section of the Republic! I was not so patriotic as to give this *strict* construction to that Palladium. I had the advantage, therefore, of others, having been schooled two whole years on the Border, previous to the outbreak.

I am constrained to hold the opinion that an ambassador to a foreign court ought to be well acquainted with the politics, manners, and customs, and particularly with the prejudices of the people with whom he is to reside, if he hopes to represent well and honorably the Government whose commission he holds. This declaration must not be met by the puerile remark, "That the analogy will not hold good!"

I maintain that institutions make a people, as much

as that a people set up institutions. And if this be true, the people of the Southern States are, to all practical purposes, *foreign* to us. Freedom is no more an institution of the North, than is Slavery an institution of the South. Toombs can lecture on the blessings of Slavery in Boston, but Sumner cannot set forth the evils of Slavery at Savannah; he is thankful when he can do this undisturbed at Washington! Now there are some foolish enough to believe that these things are not according to the "genius of our Institutions." But I maintain that they are wrong. Every man fancies that he has got "genius;" and as genius is an extraordinary endowment of nature, whereby that good dame designs to make an individual ride Jehu-like, on his own hobby—and every man on his own hobby becomes lost in admiration of the gaily-caparisoned hobby-horses of his compeers! Nature did not endow our Institutions with "genius." It was a gift made by various "geniuses." "The genius of our Institutions," is a good deal like the image of Nebuchadnezzar's dream! Be cautious you cleric! be very cautious! The reader will please bear in mind that the writer addresses himself here. "Be cautious, sir." O *my* good genius, leave me not at this trying moment! I need your help. We are in the midst of a disquisition on "genius!" My genius has consented to wait a little longer! The "genius of our Institutions" is like the image which Nebuchadnezzar saw in his dream; the huge thing which he saw in the *shape* of a man, but was not a man, was composed of materials, you know, which had no chemical affinity for each other;

to speak *ad populum*, they loved each other as oil and
water do, they would not mix, and become *something
else*.

Now, Colonel Benton, for instance, would say that
Old Hickory was well aware of this feature in our Institutions. He personified the "genius," and set the
image at his elbow, and any villain who would have
come for the purpose of dealing a blow to the clayey
toes of that incarnation of our Institutions, why he would
have heard a muttered "by the Eternal," ringing in his
ears, and flight would have been the only safety. The
"genius of our Institutions," therefore, is something like
the image. The people do not like the image as it was
compounded by our fathers. Some desire a good deal
more clay worked into the system; others think that
there is not sufficient gold in the structure of the body,
and these are very desirous to draw on California for
that precious metal; the Mariposa tract will, perhaps,
furnish a sufficient quantity. I go in for the gold, it
is *tough*. Yes, sir, tough is the word.

Well, when I was out on the Border, I had greater
necessity before me to examine the composition of the
image, which represents the "genius of our Institutions." With Captain Cuttle, of famous memory, I
"made a note of it." When I found a man who was
all gold, then an inclination of the head, as much as to
say, "Gold is the word" When another mentioned
iron, then another slight inclination, which was meant
to indicate "Iron is an excellent metal." Sometimes
we would fall in with a fellow who was all for "brass;"
this being a compound, it told me to look out for a

man who did not think that the day of compromises had gone by. " Compromises are good when well taken care of," my head would seem to nod.

The advocates of *clay, well-baked clay,* were many; to these my head would give two or three little nods, which were meant to say, "yes, have the clay well baked so as to endure for all time, *if it is a possible thing !*" I would then be asked if I did not think that the " genius of our Institutions" could be constructed of well-baked clay, so as to endure for centuries? I gently would reply, " that I *thought* not; still I was fallible, it might be so." I did not assert that it could not be so. Like Luther, I set forth the " Theses," but I *asserted* no doctrine.

This reminds me of the caption to this subject, and it also bids me give an extract from an English review, "The Christian Remembrancer," being part of a critique and analysis of the character of Martin Luther. The great man has a good character given of him in the main, but he is said to have had a great deal of *dissimulation* in his character. This charge might be brought in the same sense against the Son of God! Every effort which was made to " entangle him in his talk," was met by a wisdom which all his adversaries were not able to gainsay or resist.

Luther was endowed with some of the wisdom of his Heavenly Master; he was able for the wily diplomats of Rome. But to the interesting extract:

" But Italian policy, however sagacious and clear, had in Luther a difficult foe to deal with, and Rome was destined to find its match. The only effect which

the observation of this aim on the part of Rome had
on Luther, was to excite in him, in addition to his
original grievance, a deep and inexpressible indignation that it should be met in that way; that the only
answer to a witness against wrong should be a move
to incarcerate him. 'Was it not a shame that these
people set so high a price upon him?' He saw himself regarded as vermin, to be trodden and stamped
upon; as something whose proper fate was simple
effacement; and the bitterness of a double wrong now
invigorated and sharpened him for the contest. There
mixed with this indignation no slight disdain at the
idea that such a line of proceeding should be supposed
at all probable to succeed with him. Awake to those
vast energies which were fast rising into life within
him, and full of conscious power, he resented, while
he despised, the audacity of men who could presume
to imagine that *he* was to be caught by such strategics.
Did they think him a simpleton, or what were they
thinking of, to think that a possible thing? A mortal
jealousy of Italian subtlety only put him the more on
his mettle, and inflamed him. Luther was peculiarly
of that temper which has a horror of being taken in,
and is haunted by the '*decipi turpe est.*' The Italian
was by national character and careful cultivation a
diplomatist. He had that character, especially in Germany. The German felt himself no match for him,
and retaliated by dislike and suspicion. The dread
of an Italian was proverbial; an undefinable notion
of his unlimited powers of deception pervaded the
mass, and one German warned another as he approach-

ed. He was advancing now to the contest with his practiced penetration, his easy address, his whole art and science of management; and he promised himself an easy victory over the poor simple German. Luther's gall rose at the idea. Would he find it so easy? and would he find him quite so poor simple a German? Why should not a German assume the Italian for once, and establish some small pretension to tact and policy? It seems to have been in connection with feelings like these that Luther gave himself that *carte-blanche* for dissimulation which he used throughout all the stages of his struggle with Rome in which dissimulation was wanted. He certainly did meet the Italians here with their own weapon. He stuck at no disguises, no professions of humility, affection, reverence, and modesty, which simple language could supply, whenever his position called for them. Passion indeed is the prominent feature in Luther's character, and it does not appear at first sight as if passion and dissimulation would well go together; but they often do. Dissimulation is, after all, only a tool for accomplishing an object; and passion, which is clear-sighted enough to see this, will make use of that tool as it makes use of others. It will feel a relish in the employment of it, just as it will in the directly martial and openly hostile exercises of its calling, and even exult and triumph in it, in proportion as it is alive to its peculiar efficacy. Indeed, dissimulation will thus become a positive expression of passion; its success affords the most pungent gratification which there is to scorn, and passion specially delights in scorn; the deceiver feels that in deceiving he humiliates and degrades. Luther was as powerful a dissembler as he was an assailant. Formed just on the most formidable model in the whole workshop of character, with a degree of passion which would have driven any ordinary mortal into madness, he combined a perfect mastery and control of it, which converted it into a tool. An easy skill and a strong hand turned it about at pleasure. He did what he liked with it. He rode it as a skilful equestrian rides his high-mettled horse. He played with it as a conjuror plays with his balls, jerking and recalling them at will, and keeping them tossing in the air about him, but still obedient to the centre of attraction in himself. 'I never write so well,' he said, ' as when I am angry.' But the change from superciliousness to deference, from rage to flattery, from hatred to affection, was ready at a moment's notice, and the instrument always gave the proper note at a touch.

"With these general lines of policy prepared on both sides, hostilities commenced. The first act was a citation from the Pope to Luther to appear personally, within sixty days, at Rome. The indictments were framed; an ecclesiastical court was appointed to try his case; and the only thing wanted was the presence of the offender. 'I saw,' says Luther, ' the thunderbolt launched against me: I was the sheep that muddied the wolf's water. Tetzel escaped, and I was to let myself be eaten.' Thrown upon himself, and confronted with imminent danger thus immediately in the contest, Luther met the emergency with the utmost coolness and self-possession. There is not a symptom of its ever having entered into his head to obey the citation ; whatever happened, he had made up his mind that he would never let himself be dragged to Rome. But the resoluteness of the determination betrayed itself by no word of violence or pride.· A letter from the University of Wittemberg, with many expressions of deep reverence for the Holy See, interceded for its professor, who, ' on account of the state of his health, and the dangers attending the journey, was not able to undertake what he would otherwise be most anxious to do;' adding, ' Most holy father, our brother is indeed worthy of credit : and as for his theses against Indulgences, they are merely disputatory. He has merely exercised his right of debating freely, and has asserted nothing.' An arrangement entered into at the same time with the Elector Frederick, that the latter should decline to give Luther a safe passport to Rome, supplied him with a still more efficient and respectable excuse.

" The next attempt on the part of the Papal Court was conducted by a Nuncio in person. Cardinal Cajetan was at this time in Germany, returning from an unsuccessful mission on which he had been sent for exciting a war against the Turks. He was commissioned to undertake Luther's case, and received summary instructions ' to get hold of him, keep him safely, and bring him to Rome.'* An honest, vehement man,

---

* ' Bracchio cogas atque compellas, ut eo in potestate tuâ redacto eum sub fideli custodiâ retineas, ut coram nobis sistatur.'

without the ordinary tact of an Italian envoy, he was accompanied by an *attaché* who in some measure supplied his deficiency, Urban di Serra Longa, an Italian courtier, whose long residence in a diplomatic character in Germany had familiarized him with the national character, and made him a peculiarly fit man for dealing with a German. The Cardinal cited Luther to Augsburg; and Luther went, receiving warnings at every step to be on his guard against the sly Italians. John Kestner, of Wittemberg, provisor of the Cordeliers, was full of apprehensions for his brother— 'Thou wilt find Italians at Augsburg, brother, who are learned folks, subtle antagonists, and will give thee a great deal of trouble. I fear thou wilt not be able to maintain thy cause against them; they will throw thee in the fire, and consume thee in the flames.' Doctor Auerbach, of Leipsic, repeated the note of warning—'The Italians are not to be trusted.' Prebend Adelmann, of Leipsic, repeated it after him. There was small need for impressing it upon Luther. Arrived at Augsburg, he was waited on by Serra Longa, who took the line of advising him, as a sensible man, to submit himself to the Cardinal without reserve. 'Come,' he concluded, 'the Cardinal is waiting for you. I will escort you to him myself. Fear nothing; all will be over soon, and without difficulty.' Luther heard him with respect, and expressed himself as perfectly ready to meet the Cardinal; but he wanted one thing before doing so—a safe conduct. 'A safe conduct? Do not think of asking for one; the legate is well disposed, and quite ready to end the affair amicably. If you ask for a safe conduct, you will spoil your business.' The *attaché's* assurance was confirmed by the rest of the Cardinal's suite: 'The Cardinal assures you of his grace and favor;' 'the Cardinal is a father, full of compassion.' Luther expressed no distrust in him, but wanted a safe conduct.

"The safe conduct came, and Luther presented himself before the Cardinal, secure and humble. Prostrating himself first, he waited for one command to raise him to his knees, and another to raise him to his legs. After a silence, in which the Cardinal expected him to speak, but Luther humbly waited to be addressed, the conference commenced. Cajetan was stern, brief, and summary, and simply demanded retractation. Luther required argument to prove that he was wrong. For several successive interviews the same game went on, and Luther suggested argument, and the Cardinal repelled it. As Luther, however, remained cool, while the Cardinal became angry and heated, the balance of the discussion at last inclined in the former's favor, and he caught the Cardinal in a trap,—one sufficiently frivolous, indeed, but according to the technical laws of logic acknowledged in that day, decisive argumentatively. One of Luther's objectionable theses was, that 'the treasure of Indulgences was not composed of the merits and sufferings of our Lord Jesus Christ.' The Cardinal asserted this to be flatly contradictory to the *extravagante* of Pope Clement. Luther challenged him to prove it, and the challenge was caught eagerly. The *extravagante* was produced and read till they came to the words 'the

Lord Jesus Christ has *acquired* the treasure by his sufferings.' 'Pause there,' said Luther. 'Most reverend father, be good enough carefully to consider and reflect on that phrase, "He has *acquired*." Christ has acquired a treasure by his merits; the merits, therefore, are not the treasure; for, to speak with philosophers, the cause is different from the things which flow from it.' Cajetan had committed a mistake in being enticed into an argument, and did not regain his position.

" Luther, having puzzled the Cardinal, and done all he had to do; having noticed, too, symptoms of irascibility in his judge, from whom he began to receive first offers and then threats of a safe conduct to Rome, resolved to take his leave; leaving with his friends, first, a note to the Cardinal, explaining that the smallness of his resources did not allow him to protract his stay in Augsburg; and, secondly, an appeal to the Pope, whereby the Cardinal's hands were tied, and any retaliatory sentence to which his offended dignity might incline him, stopped. Before the morning light he-mounted a horse, issued out of a small gate in the city, which a town-councillor had directed to be open for him, and left Augsburg at a gallop. His feelings on his return to Wittemberg were those of bitter merriment, not softened by the sight, which he then for the first time had, of the written directions contained in the Pope's brief to the Cardinal. 'The Cardinal would fain have had me in his hands, and sent me to Rome. He is vexed, I warrant, that I have escaped him. He fancied he was master of me in Augsburg;

he thought he had me; but he had got the eel by the tail.'"

I trust that the insertion of this passage, to point my moral, will not be regarded as a piece of folly and presumption. I took Luther for a model in diplomacy, in the same sense that artists take Titian for a model as a painter; there has been but one Titian, and I "reckon" that Luther will not lose his identity; but if I should turn out a rival, my biographers—for, in that case, I shall have biographers—will attend to the whole matter, and see that I shall not suffer by the comparison!

Now, the end of the whole of this chapter is just simply this: I was permitted to remain on the Border, "*closely watched*," until the fever and ague took hold of me, and then it was wisely concluded that I could do but little harm, as I was unable to *preach!*

CHAPTER XXII.

The subject of this chapter has had more "honors thrust upon him," than generally falls to the lot of individuals. He has been designated General Stringfellow, Lawyer Stringfellow, Doctor String-fellow, "Speaker of the House of Delegates of the Missouri-Kansas-Legislature-Stringfellow " " Vestry-man Stringfellow." He has also been invested with something like ubiquity;—some make him reside in Missouri—some, in Kansas. Now, I wish to say to the world, that this is not fair. It is utterly impossible that B. F. S. could attend to all these matters, and whip Gov. Reeder into the bargain. There are two brothers by the name of Stringfellow. "Simeon and Levi are brethren; instruments of cruelty are in their habita-tions." I presume that the confusion of the two per-sonages in one, arises from the fact that the *principal calling of both* is sufficient to make them lose their iden-tity! They are both disposed to do all they can for the "goose," and more than most men would do, or would dare to do, unless they had good backers.

But let us divide the honors. B. F. Stringfellow is a lawyer—he is called General by courtesy, I believe;

he was a vestryman, and perhaps is now in that office, in a parish, founded by myself, at Weston, Mo. He resides at Weston, Mo.

J. H. Stringfellow, brother of B. F. S., is a Doctor and an Editor, and was the Speaker of the House of Delegates in Kansas. He resides at Atchison, K. T. The Doctor is a member of the M. E. Church, South.

Neither of these gentlemen ever offered me violence. This is saying a great deal. I once received a personal introduction to the Doctor, in days long past, before the science of "gooseology" came into fashion; but, since that time,

> "A glance from his eye,
> Shun danger, and fly,"

was the rule with me.

B. F. S. I knew much better than I did his brother, though no person would ever do me the favor to present me to him. He did not reside at Weston, during my first stay in the country. When I returned, he was then settled at this point. The "goose" interposed—I wore no "hemp" in my button-hole; consequently, I was never presented. But B. F. S. and myself often talked, in a *mixed* company.

Gen. Stringfellow is, perhaps, forty-seven years of age; he is five feet six inches high, florid complexion, yellow hair.

It was always my impression that he was a good-tempered man. Every morning he would pass down by the door of the house at which I at one time resided, leisurely and slowly, and meditatively, with his pipe in his mouth; his head would become enveloped in a cloud of smoke. You see, he did not walk fast enough to leave one puff behind him, ere another puff came; "and a-puffing he would go," until he got down to the door of the "St. George Hotel," directly opposite his own office; and there would be found a chair, and there would be clients, and there would be "squatter sovereigns," and there would be couriers from the Territory, and there would be editors of "Platte Arguses" and "Leavenworth Heralds;" and, occasionally, the voice of "Davy" would discourse the "Music of the Border," coming down the street, on his way from Platte City. Davy would throw the reins on the neck of his steed, and the black boy would take him to the stable. Davy would say · "Well, Ben, what's the news?" If he received an answer, he would have to go quite close to Ben, to learn its nature. Ben was very much indisposed to exertion. He talked very much at his case—he did everything at his ease; he published a pamphlet very much at his ease, entitled, "Negro Slavery no Evil." I compared its statistics with those in the Census Reports, but they did not agree; and I agreed not to state my discoveries. I had private reasons. I merely concluded that Ben had consulted his ease more than the Census, in making out his case. I never was more surprised, than when I heard that B. F. S. was going to shoot Gov. Reeder. I may not understand the character of B. F. S., but if I am mistaken, the most of his friends have the same opinion of him that I have. For instance, he has a distant relative, living at Kickapoo City, who was a member of the Kansas Legislature at the time; well, I never saw, or heard, man laugh more heartily than did this man, at the idea of B. F. S. fighting with Gov. Reeder. I do not mean to say that B. F. S. is not good in council. He has shown himself good in giving bad counsel, more than once; but it may be relied on, that he will leave the execution to others.

There was once, however, a time when the General, in obedience to the advice of Mr. Toots, "made an effort."

The nomination of a candidate to represent the people of Kansas, was appointed to take place, once upon a time. The people of Missouri where I lived, showed a lively interest in the matter. They felt disposed to lend a helping hand on such occasions. This meeting was to be held at Leavenworth City. It was the time when Whitfield was re-nominated.

Many were the men at Weston this day, on horseback, having on their dragoon coats. There was something in the wind, I was sure. I took a careless walk down past the "St. George." Ben was just tapping the ashes out of his pipe—making his thumb-nail the anvil on which he smote the instrument. He had his dragoon coat on, and the horse was standing at the door. The Statesman mounted, sat. An irregular cavalcade went down to the ferry-boat, lying about a mile below the town. I walked down towards the boat, and as I walked, James Burns, Esq., of Weston, whom I liked, overtook me on horseback. He addressed me, and asked me to take a notice, which he handed me, and put it up in a public place, on board of one of the Missouri River Packets, which was lying about a quarter of a mile below Weston.

I took the notice; it was a declinature of a nomination for Congress, on the part of James, and was designed, of course, to notify those on board of that boat, who were residents of Weston, and its neighborhood, and on their way down to the meeting, to be held at Leavenworth, K. T.

I went on board the boat and asked a gentleman to put up the notice. I found Parson Kerr on board, from Fort Leavenworth. He had a few copies of his pamphlet in defence of Slavery with him, which he had circulated among the faithful on board. The Parson never gave me a copy of his pamphlet, although we were very intimate with each other. I stepped out of the cabin and stood talking with a gentleman for a moment at the door of the cabin, outside; while here, and almost instantly after I left the cabin, a gentleman who, at that time, had just come from some of the lower counties of Missouri, Russell by name, and now of the famous firm of "Major & Russell," at Leavenworth City, came out, having been advised thereto by Parson K., to look at me in a contemptuous manner, and to take the dimensions of a little Parson not sound on the "goose." Mr. R. looked at me, and I looked at him. Some of the brethren will tell me "that I had no business there." And there is a great deal of philosophy in the observation, about as much as there was in a remark made by a man who had the Government contract to supply the Indians with flour, up in the Kansas country, when expostulated with for cheat-

ing the poor creatures ; he replied, " They have no business to be Indians !"

Well, Ben laid aside his pipe, mounted his horse
and accompanied by many valiant men, went down to
take care of the interest of the people of Kansas.
" As goes the Empire State, so goes the Union." As
goes Weston, so goes Kansas ! Whitfield was nominated, and a nomination was just the same as an election.
I have not taken much interest in politics since I left
Kansas, but I believe Whitfield did not serve out his
term.

CHAPTER XXIII.

FOR several days previous to the 30th of March, 1855, the day on which the members for the Legislature in Kansas were to be chosen, there were *very decided* evidences to be seen in Missouri, of the paternal interest which her people took in Kansas affairs. "Self-Defensives" met at Platte City—"Self-Defensives" met at Weston—"Self-Defensives" met at Leavenworth. "The Platte Argus" gave in its colums the "general" orders from head-quarters. Saddle-horses were all engaged *for the day of invasion*. Tents were in process of being constructed in almost every house, for the boys. All the old dragoon coats were borrowed. Shot guns, rifles, revolvers, and bowie knives were borrowed for the occasion. Whiskey canteens and bottles were borrowed; numerous orders were sent in to the saddlers for straps to hang the canteens over the shoulders of the volunteers. I merely state here what came under my own observation. I could not be in fifty places at the same time. I take no hearsay reports to guide my pen.

Everything depended upon the point of destination which had been assigned to the different corps of the boys. I mean, if A.'s company was designed to carry

[142]

the polls at Marysville, on the Big Blue, why, then, Mr. A. must start at least five days before the opening of the polls. If B.'s company had been ordered to take Leavenworth by storm, why then B. could wait until the last moment, and go down to the sound of "*fife and drum.*"

On the day previous to the election, a party of the "Platte County Boys" came into Weston, for the most part on horseback, but some in wagons. They had tufts of hemp (the staple of Platte County) in their hats and in their button holes. This party had a long pole surmounted by the *animal alive and squawking!* This animal was not the bird of Jove, but the bird of the barn-yard—reader, it was "the goose!" From henceforth let this animal be mentioned with honor. O ye future historians, give it a place in your annals; when you mention "Roman Eagles," say a word in behalf of "Missouri Geese!"

The party which had the "goose" alive and kicking —no she was not kicking—her feet were strapped to the pole, this might have been emblematic of Slavery, the object of the conquest of Kansas—but we rather think that the object was to keep "mother goose" in *subjection,* or better yet, in *elevation!*—the party, then, which had the "goose" alive and *not* kicking, crossed the Rubicon on the day previous to the battle. I do not know where they camped, and anxiously hoped for the morrow. Somebody else, perhaps, can follow the line of march and the engagement which took place at the ballot-box, by which the "goose" ruined Kansas, as a set-off to the salvation of Rome, by the cackling of "geese." You cannot rely upon geese any more than you can upon men. They will stultify them-selves. But perhaps the geese on the Kansas border had never read of the patriotism of their ancestry at Rome. Or if this is too great a reflection, perhaps they had forgotten. Men forget, and arguing from analogy, geese will forget too.

Pay-day will come, and the 30th of March, 1855, came. The "Weston Band" discoursed its music. An army of *Infantry* collected. A line was formed of those *who affected* to love slavery, but who loved whiskey with an unfeigned love.

"March! March! rummies in order, March!"

This company embarked for Leavenworth. I do not know what they did there, except I credit what many of them said they did—"gave in their votes for the Pro-Slavery candidates." I am induced to believe that they told the truth; but the reader must judge for himself; there was nothing to prevent them from voting at Leavenworth that day.

My reader will bear in mind, that there were two ferry-boats running between the neighborhood of Wes-ton and the Kansas shore. As a matter of course, these boats, if personified, were rivals. John Wells owned the steam ferry-boat which plied between the Rialto, a landing a little below Weston, and the landing on the opposite Kansas shore, only three miles from Fort Leavenworth. John Wells had always been sound on the "bird" above alluded to—not a breath of suspicion ever entered the minds of any, with reference to "J. W."

But two miles above Weston, opposite Kickapoo, there plied a long-low-dilapidated-suspicious-looking-flat-boat, John Ellis, Commander.

John was originally from Hoosierdom, but had long dwelt on the bottom land of the Missouri, in the famed Platte Purchase. He had simply, on the passage of the Kansas Bill, moved his traps from the east bank to the west bank of the Missouri, and went into the flat-boat carrying trade. The business remunerated, or John would not have continued it. He had been in successful operation, as a ferryman, for several months previous to the day of the election for the members of the Legislature. J. E., at this time, was about forty-five years of age, perhaps; he looked older, but he had used himself badly. He was small of stature; his complexion was *quite florid*—he painted in whiskey colors. His nose was a little aquiline, having quite extended and flabby nostrils—color, *à la* turkey-gobbler's gills. Oh, John, forgive me; you know my profession, I cannot paint you, conscientiously, in anything but *true* colors; but, John, I owe you many thanks. Many a time did John wade into the water, up to his knees, to take me in his embrace, and place me gently in his flat-boat, when I wanted to cross over, to preach at Kickapoo. Perhaps, John, the New York Society Library will get a copy of this little book, and then you will be rendered immortal! I must acknowledge that this portrait will do you no *good*, until *after you are dead!* but if, after you are dead and gone, you will "still live," then, John, I shall have repaid your many kindnesses, with interest.

But, John, I have not done with you yet. Your heart was good, but your conscience was of the India-rubber order. John, did you not, for six months previous to this election day, quietly and diplomatically interrogate every *bona fide* immigrant which you took over in your boat, what his opinion was on the prospect of Slavery, or no Slavery, in Kansas? Did you not find, at least, five out of every seven of these heads of families determined to vote " No Slavery ?" Ah, John ! to comfort me, you told me this. I did not ask your opinion, John ; but you *guessed* that the news would be acceptable to me, and you imparted it. But the "Self-Defensives" found you out, John. "Put no money in John Ellis's purse," was the word.

But, behold, an invading army had to be crossed over the Missouri. John took a view of the camp. A quarter of a dollar, each way (of course, they would all come back again !) for a man and horse—and a dollar for every wagon. " There is no use in talking, these fellows will all get over, and they will all come back again, and their money is as good as that of anybody's else." John parleyed with Satan, and was outwitted. John hastened down to the office of the " Platte Argus," in Weston, and had a notice printed, precisely setting forth the following declaration :

" Some illy-disposed persons have tried to injure my ferry, by stating that I refused to cross persons, last fall, to go to the election. This is false ;—it will be difficult to find one more sound on the ' goose,' than I am

"(Signed,)   JOHN ELLIS."

This placard I read, where it was tacked up, on the side of the flat-boat. The business of John largely increased. A steam ferry-boat took the place of the flat, in a short time. This shows the importance of advertising!

CHAPTER XXIV.

DISCRETION THE BETTER PART OF VALOR.

A BUGGY stood one Saturday afternoon in front of a store, in Weston; the shafts of this vehicle aided by the harness, *held up* an apology for a horse! The buggy at this time was full of sundries; a bag of corn-meal, several small packages of tea, sugar, coffee, &c., cooking utensils, such as a coffee-pot, frying-pan, a few camp platters, made of tin, and other little notions, too numerous to mention. I inquired whose establishment this was? I was answered that it belonged to Dr. Lieb, of Leavenworth. I waited until I saw the Doctor. In one moment I will tell the reader why I wished to see him. I desired to preach at Leavenworth, the next day, eight miles distant. I had intended walking down. If I had hired a horse on that Saturday, P. M., the charge would have been one dollar for that afternoon, two dollars for the next day, and one dollar for the return on Monday morning; ferriage both ways fifty cents; livery for the horse a day and two nights, one dollar and fifty cents; my own bill at the hotel for a day and a half, three dollars; a sum total of nine dollars! The clergy will understand what this exclamation point means, better than W. B. Astor.

"Now," said I to myself, "if I can just get in with

the Doctor, and be trundled along on the level part of the road, I will walk up hill, and on Monday I will have all day to walk back; the expense under these favorable circumstances would only be three dollars and twenty cents, and this I had to pay out of my own pocket.

The Doctor is now approaching. " Doctor, I would like to go down to Leavenworth with you?" Those who have ever seen the Doctor, will at once fancy the nervous twitch which he gave his shoulder when this question was propounded. The Doctor replied, " That the horse belonged to Mr. Smith, missionary among the Delawares," and referred me to the condition of the beast. I told him " that I would walk up hills, if he could let me go with him." Another twitch of the shoulder, and a " Well," from his tongue. It was settled.

" Poor as a church mouse," has got to be stale—for a novelty, and which will be as equally true, let there be a variation · " As dilapidated as a missionary's horse."

Dr. Lieb was a Pennsylvanian, but had lately been in Iowa. This latter State was too far advanced to permit of an opportunity to mend his fallen fortunes, so he came to Kansas; clean linen, the texture, the color of other garments, or the fashionable cuts, or nice adjustment of the whole to the human frame, were matters of "no consequence." The Doctor enjoyed the freedom of the border in all these particulars, to the full extent of the " Common Law." In person, the Doctor was very large and fleshy. The seat of the buggy was all occupied by him, save a small corner of it on which I could lean, but not sit. Every minute or two the Doctor would make his nervous lurch, and so ponderous was the mountain of flesh thus made to quiver, that the vehicle would shake to its very centre, and the poor old horse would careen to either side!

I think that I have before hinted that the Doctor could enjoy a large quantity of "Bourbon," without being overcome. His philanthropy, however, was called into play in behalf of all those who could *not* thus endure and conquer: "*Vincit qui patitur,*" was the Doctor's motto.

The Doctor was advertised to deliver a Temperance Lecture at the Presbyterian Church in Weston, Mis- souri! This was an attempt to carry the war into Africa, but it was not carried.

During the interval between the announcement of the anticipated effort on the part of the Doctor, to re- trieve his fellow ————s, and the evening on which the rostrum was to have been occupied by the orator, office had sought the Doctor. Governor Reeder had appointed the Doctor to take the census of the Leaven- worth and other districts in the Territory. Of course the "Self-Defensives" said that nobody could be ap- pointed by the Governor, unless he was an Abolitionist!

The Doctor was now to be received in Weston as an official of Governor Reeder should be.

The church bell rang for the temperance lecture. I went over to the church. The odor of pitch pervaded the street—the tar was seething, and the bag of feathers lay ready to deck a bird who stood in need of plum- age!

We waited and waited in the church; finally the Rev. Mr. Starr, the pastor, with a mischievous twinkle in his eye, and a smile all over him, "presumed that other pressing duties had deprived the assembly of the pleasure of hearing Doctor Lieb, on a subject, for the discussion of which he was well qualified; he would not, however, dismiss the audience, but would entertain them as well as he could be expected to do on so short a notice."

It would never have done for Mr. Starr to have announced having received a communication from the Doctor, telling them that he would be obliged to disappoint them. Oh no; the best way was to let the matter go by default! Leave it to the imagination of each.

My impression was that the Doctor, being acquainted with drugs and such like essences, had smelt tar, even across the river; but I was afterwards informed that a friend had informed him of the honor which awaited him, and that he had resolved to decline it.

CHAPTER XXV.

W. P. R. has been for many years a resident of St. Joseph, Mo. He is a large property holder. He is a frontiers-man in every sense of the term. He was Indian Agent for several tribes during the administration of Taylor and Fillmore. He is the father-in-law of a late Member of Congress from the Platte district. Among all my acquaintances on the border, I do not know of one who would carry the law of brutality so far in forcing slavery upon the people of Kansas, as W. P. R. He is a large, fierce-looking man, long accustomed to kick and cuff poor negroes and Indians, and abominates an anti-slavery white man more than he does either negro or Indian. I have learned, not many weeks past, from a highly-respectable clergyman of our Episcopal church, who had the best opportunity to know the facts, that W. P. R. consulted with those who love me on the border, what had better be done with me.

This is the only instance wherein *actual personal abuse* and *decidedly brutal* treatment had ever been advised to be exercised *towards me* while I lived on the border. Yes, the author of the " Black Statute" in the so-called Kansas Laws, was the only one who ever

[152]

offered to maltreat an inoffensive, weak, afflicted minister of his own church!! The author of the Black
Law—the law declared by almost every Senator in
Congress, even from the South—yes, by the Senator
from South Carolina, Mr. Butler, a disgrace to the age,
a disgrace even to the Slave States themselves, was the
man who would have had me, while I was lying sick
at St. Joseph, and watched and nursed by slaveholders,
this man would have had me taken off my sick-bed
and tarred and feathered, and it may be, murdered!
Oh, merciful God, is this the man who now is called
General of the Militia of Kansas,—yes, who is at this
moment in which I write, collecting a wild set of men
to murder the few Free State settlers of Kansas!

If the "Genius of Liberty" were the meekest, the
sweetest, and the purest, and the loveliest of virgins,
and she should be sitting disconsolate by a log hut
weeping and bewailing her condition on the plains of
Kansas; and if accosted by W. P. R., and asked,
"Woman, why weepest thou?" and she should answer,
"because they have taken away and murdered the
last defender of Liberty on this soil," then that man
would, with delight, spring from his horse, and throttle
that loveliest of beings, simply because she was the
Genius of Liberty!

I write that here which, before my God, I solemnly
believe! The black and cruel Law in the Draco-
Kansas Code, is but the index of the black brutality
of its author's heart. Come, sir, and kill me; and the
last moment of time to me will be the happiest, for I
shall feel that Kansas will indeed be free!

7*

W.—orthy P.—rince R.—uffian, is this General of the Kansas Militia. Cruel and bloody times will have made this man's name a stench in the nostrils of the latest posterity in the Western country.

CHAPTER XXVI.

THIS chapter will contain a grave charge against a man in public life.

There was issued at Parkville, in Platte County, in the State of Missouri, a paper called the "Parkville Luminary." It was edited by a gentleman by the name of Patterson: the proprietor of the paper was named Park, a very influential and respectable man, and long a resident in Missouri,—in fact, the substantial town of Parkville had been named after Mr. Park. I used to read this paper regularly. There were enterprising men at the head of it. They had made arrangements for the reception of telegraphic despatches directly to them from St. Louis and the East, on current events,—a very rare circumstance for country newspaper publishers, particularly in Missouri. This paper always advocated the institutions of the South and of the State of Missouri; but one unfortunate mistake it made. Just after the election in Kansas, it gave forth to the world its opinion that it was not right for the people of Missouri to go over and vote at elections in Kansas. Now this was treason to the institution of Slavery! It was worse than Abolition; it was a leader of public opinion, telling the people that it was wrong to force the institution of Slavery upon a people who did not want it! The "Self-Defensives" were called in council, and the destruction of the Press, and the banishment of its editors and proprietors, determined upon, and carried into effect. I assert here, without fear of contradiction, that the Constitution of the United States was violated in the destruction of the press, and in the expatriation of the above-named gentlemen, for the sole reason that in their responsible position they counselled righteousness! Bear this in mind, for I wish to show you a man who offered to reward the iniquity.

My wife and myself were on board of the steamboat Polar Star, on the Missouri river. Dr. Bonnifant, of Weston, and many others whom I knew, were there. The boat was a public place of resort; there was a large crowd of passengers. At Kansas City there came on board a tall, wiry-looking man, about forty years of age, perhaps. There is nothing intellectual looking about him. He has a dull gray eye, coarse, sand-colored hair, very ordinary in every respect. This is J. W. Whitfield, late Indian Agent, and late M. C., but at the time of which I am writing, strong in his assurance of holding his seat in Congress.

Now, nobody could believe otherwise than that this gentleman had been put in nomination by the "Weston Regency"—I never believed, for nobody in Weston ever tried to make me believe, otherwise. The truth is, it was a piece of good news in Weston, too good to be kept, it was in everybody's mouth. The "Weston Regency" nominated Whitfield, and the "Weston Regency" effected his election,—he was the Pro-Slavery candidate; the name of democrat never entered into either of the plans for nomination, or of those for election. But when J. W. Whitfield got to Washington, there was some anxiety to learn on what issue he had been elected in Kansas? The friends of the Kansas Bill got it through the House of Representatives, by giving the assurance that Kansas could never become anything else but a Free State; but behold Whitfield comes, having been sent to Congress by Pro-Slavery men, to advocate Pro-Slavery interests! What is to be done? Why, let Harry Hibbard, of New Hampshire, address a letter to Whitfield, inquiring on what issue he had been elected, and let Whitfield write in reply, that he was elected on the "National Democratic issue," i. e., the Baltimore Platform issue: "Let Slavery alone." We shall take you at your word, Mr. Whitfield. I will hold you to it, for I want to pin to you a stigma unworthy an honest man. But just for the moment let me remark, that for this letter to Harry Hibbard, you come pretty near being shelved by the "Weston Regency." The "Platte Argus" came down on you, Mr. Whitfield; it declared, when it first published your letter, that you were elected on the Pro-Slavery issue, and none other. And the "Argus" was right. But, nevertheless, I am also bound to take you at your word. You have written that you were elected as a "National Democrat"—as one who reveres the very letters, and jots and tittles of that Constitution, as much as ever old Jew did the letters or points of the Hebrew Bible,—and yet, Mr. J. W. Whitfield did loudly, and before his own family, and before the family of Dr. Bonnifant, and in my hearing, and with a glance directed towards where I sat at table, declare the people of Parkville did well when they destroyed the press of the Luminary; and I, for one, will give twenty-five dollars towards procuring a medal for them, to commemorate the deed!

This is the truth, reader: must there not, then, be great morality, much religion, abundance of patriotism, in that upper country?

Pooh, pooh! we do not go to priests to learn politics! Neither do I go to dishonest political quacks, to get my divinity or morality. Tyranny, bloodshed, and civil war, come under *my* catalogue of crimes—and Slavery is the cause of these three crimes, being perpetrated on the border at this moment. If this is "National Democracy," then I will also add it to the list of crimes.

CHAPTER XXVII.

DEVELOPMENT—A NEW ARTICLE REQUIRED IN THE CREED.

THE liberties of the Church, and the liberties of the State, if not identical, are closely allied. If either is dependent on the other, then the liberties of the Church occupy the subordinate position. In countries where the Church and the State are united, there the politics are common. A statesman is a churchman, and a churchman is a politician. This state of things is unavoidable. For instance, in Great Britain, what Church act does not receive the sanction of a lay parliament, or what purely State act does not receive the assent of the Bench of Bishops ; or, if the question be on the rejection of a measure, either of an ecclesiastical or of a secular nature, it must be rejected by the influence of both Church and State.

We have no such union of State and Church in the United States : very true, we have no particular body of professed Christian people recognized as the Church of the nation ; but the united body of professed Christian people constitute this nation, with comparatively few exceptions—the only difference is, that a profession of Christianity is not made a test for the enjoyment of any right or privilege of a purely political nature. There is, then, an inseparable union of Christianity and the State, even in these United States.

As a professor of Christ's religion, or as both a professor and a teacher of the doctrines of the cross, a citizen of this Union has a profound interest in every important measure of the government. A flippant, empirical journalist will tell us, with a flourish of trumpets, "that we do not go to the pulpit to learn politics." I for one reply, that I do not go to the "American Congress," or to any other Legislative body under heaven, for my "Moral Law"—this or that body cannot determine for me what is *sin*, or what is not—what shall be subjects for discourse to my people, or what shall be forbidden doctrine!

Now, my conscience has satisfied both my head and my heart, that the State has been circumscribing Christianity in its onward march of peace and love to *all men*, for many years past, but within these few years most undoubtedly.

There has been development in the State, on a subject which involves in jeopardy almost every point of God's law! Is African slavery in America a blessing? It has been legislated upon as if it were; therefore, the policy of the State is conducted on this hypothesis. African slavery in the United States is a blessing *according to law!* Christianity, through her teachers, is invoked to endorse this manifesto. Is the Church prepared for the question?

I have made myself familiar with the records of history, with reference to human slavery. I have studied the subject in the Old Testament—there are

texts therein which teach nothing else but abolition. I
have often considered the passages in the New Testament, which recognize the existence of a bondage by
law, which *law Christians never made!* I know the
history of the introduction of African slavery into
these States when they were colonies ; and one of the
charges which is made in the Declaration of Independence against the tyrant of the Colonies is, that "he has
forced Slavery upon us !" I have read the Declaration of Independence, and I find a sentiment at war
with chattel slavery—"all men are created equal," and
the clause which follows this declaration contains its
exegesis—"life, liberty, and the pursuit of happiness, are inalienable rights." I send to the wind the
profane and absurd interpolation of these degenerate
days· " All *white* men .only are contemplated!" Supremely ridiculous ! Why did not the patriots insert
the word *white,* as our model legislators do, in this day
of progress backwards?

I have read the Constitution of the United States,
and I wish to interpret it as its framers understood it.
That the article in the instrument which declares the
" persons held to service," &c., has reference to fugitive
slaves, I never had a doubt, although, for wise and
good purposes, the word slave does not disgrace the
Constitution. I regret the existence of Slavery, and
of course I regret the temporary moral necessity of the
rendition of fugitive slaves; but, though it is a law which
makes every good Christian man sigh—until God shall
provide differently, let good patriots and statesmen of
all parties do justice, with mercy, in this matter.

In addition to my reading and the study of the fore-mentioned history and instruments, I have traced the sentiments of the patriots of the past; and the result of my labors is the firm conviction, "that the founders of this Government regarded Slavery as a canker which was to be kept at all hazards from spreading to the vitals of the body politic."

Now, it will at once be obvious that under such a conviction, and with such a policy as is indicated above, neither the duties of a minister of God, nor the desires of a true philanthropist, would ever be obstructed. The amelioration of the evil Slavery would be as proper a subject for treatment, as that of any other existing evil.

But at this day everything is changed in the political world. Slavery is now a blessing, and must be extended by law and by force of arms! The Church may endorse the Constitution of the United States, take the Declaration of Independence and make it her own; but is she prepared to waive her right to say that the bloody code of Kansas, and such like legislation, is at war with the rights of mankind and subversive of the teachings of Christ?

Will the Protestant Episcopal Church, in whose bosom a Washington was nurtured, surrender her high prerogative in the tremendous question which agitates at this time the moral world?

This great, conservative, and highly-esteemed Church, in whose collective capacity I was an officer and a minister; whose commission to preach the Gospel of Christ I received at the hands of one of our Southern Bishops, acting in behalf of a Northern Bishop; has

not had the power to sustain me in Kansas, or to commend me successfully to the few members of our
Church there, simply because I did not in my conscience believe Slavery a blessing, and worthy of extension. If a more heinous charge than this can be
brought against me, I desire to be put on trial. I
challenge investigation. My witnesses shall be Slaveholders themselves, on the Borders of Kansas!

I was told by a clergyman of our own Church, not
two months since, that they are now writing East from
one of the towns situated not more than seven miles
from my former place of residence in Kansas, and
a town in which I was well known, and expressing a
desire to have a clergyman sent to them who will be
in favor of Slavery! The Presbyterian Church at St.
Joseph advertised for a Pastor, stating that if the applicant should be a Northern man he must have
Southern principles! The Rev. F. Starr, Presbyterian
Pastor at Weston, Mo., for seven years, which length
of residence proves clearer than would a score of affi-
davits, that he was not a fanatic nor an incendiary, was
obliged, when the Kansas question came up, to leave
Weston, because he could not conscientiously say "God
speed" to the introduction of Slavery into that Territory, by force and fraud! I was not forcibly expelled
from the country, but the effort to do so was suggested
in more than one meeting of influential men,—my
letters were robbed, my plans for Church extension
were crushed, places wherein to preach the Gospel
were denied me, the owners being impelled to refuse,
as they told me, through fear, and all this and many

more acts of oppression were exercised towards me, for the simple reason above stated.

When I went to Kansas my heart and my conscience alone were for freedom—and the heart and the conscience of all our clergy, with a few ignoble exceptions, are in favor of freedom,—but now my conscience, my heart, my head, my tongue, my pen, and if need be, my life, are at the service of Freedom!

Is the doctrine of Slavery extension *implicitly* held in the Church? This dogma was required from me, I maintain, by friends and members of our communion on the Border, as a condition on which alone I could preach the Gospel to them. Leading statesmen in the Southern States, who maintain that Slavery is a blessing, are selected to represent their Dioceses in our General Convention: this is all very well if they in their heart believe that Slavery is a blessing, I cannot change their mind or interfere with their conscience, but I do wish to know whether they are determined to make their ideas articles of the faith? For no less importance can be attached to the conduct of the Borderers, in my practical expulsion from Kansas, than that a belief in *Slavery extension* should be an article of the creed!

If our clergy do not chafe the consciences of the Slaveholder in the South by their public teachings, then I think, at least, the laity should, in return for the kindness, allow a narrow-minded clergyman to enjoy his private opinion on this subject of Slavery.

Our Church bears a wonderful analogy in her government and in her union to that of the State in these

United States,—*E Pluribus Unum* is applicable to her now, and may it be perpetually so. But the liberty of prophesying is infinitely more in danger in the States of the Church at the North, than are the liberties of the people in the Northern Civil States from the aggression of the South.

Our Legislative bodies consist of a House of Bishops, a Bishop from every State or Diocese,—this is our Senate,—and a House of Clerical and Lay Deputies, consisting of four clergymen and four laymen from every State or Diocese,—this is our House of Representatives.

The reader will perceive that there is not representation according to the number of the inhabitants of the diocese, or according to the number of the members, or of the clergy in the different dioceses; but, simply and solely, on the number of the dioceses.

For instance, the diocese of Arkansas, with its six or eight clergymen, and a few hundred communicants, has as much influence, in legislation for the Church, as the diocese of New York, with its hundreds of clergymen, and its tens of thousands of communicants.

If the doctrine of Slavery extension is implicitly held in our Church, there is nothing to hinder the *explicit* setting of it forth, as a doctrine, and the addition of a new article to the creed.

It can be accomplished, at any time, when a general convention meets. The best of all laws, the law of prudence and propriety, has kept this subject of Slavery out of the Episcopal Church; but if this vile thing, once a degraded servant, now attempts to Lord it in Church and

State—causing civil war in the State, and mean, petty persecutions in the Church—will anybody tell me where our safety lies? Shall I be told that the Church has nothing to fear, because the slaveholders who belong to the Church, and legislate for the Church, are men who are pious, or piously disposed, and, consequently, *must regard* Slavery as an evil, to be tolerated solely, by us, the people of God, as God himself tolerates and bears with a thousand evils? Surely, if this were the sentiment, I should have been allowed to preach the Gospel undisturbed, on the Border, when I held in my hand the commission from a standing committee of the whole Church, and recommended to that committee by a Bishop, who has known me from the day I first be· gan my studies for the ministry. There are just such men in the South, as, for instance, Adam Beatty, Esq., of Kentucky, a churchman who has represented the Diocese of Kentucky in General Convention, who is at this moment writing for liberty of speech in that State; but let him beware, or leave, unless, indeed, Kentucky is tired of Slavery; and if so, then a great additional reason is given to us why it should not be extended.

But, where there is one Adam Beatty, there are ten thousand such churchmen as the Governor of Virginia, or as my communicant, Major Maclin, of the Border.

After all our talking, and writing, and preaching, and fighting, there are but two sides to this question. Slavery is either a blessing, or it is a curse; if it is a blessing, let it be so stated; if it is an evil, let it be placed in the catalogue of evils, to be endured until it can, with safety, and moderation, and justice, be cured. I place it in this latter category; but I cannot preach the Gospel on the Border, with these sentiments, unless I go and throw myself into the arms of the Free State settlers, and take my revolver in my hand, to protect my life. I tell you, brethren in the Gospel ministry, this is the solemn and awful truth.

Are not the liberties of the Church in danger, then? Is not the moral law of God in danger, as far as His law can be placed in danger, by the issue which I am considering. Is not Slavery a prime source of every crime forbidden in the Decalogue. This is true, and the good people of the South have often told me as much; but I did not need to be told—I have seen it, I know it; and it cannot be otherwise.

Let a new article be set forth in the creed, then, that simple-minded clergymen from the North, who feel disposed to preach the Gospel of Christ in a Southern State, from whatever motive that is good—it may be, because his constitution requires a milder climate—so that his conscience may be set at rest, when he shall see the thousand ills of Slavery, by turning simply to the creed, and there this Slavery shall be found classed among the fundamentals of Christianity!

St. Bernard once preached against a greater absurdity than Slavery; and one, for the setting forth of which nothing whatever could be gathered from the Scriptures—I refer to the doctrine of the "Immaculate Conception of the Virgin Mother;" and yet we have lived to see this set forth by the whole Roman Catholic world, in 1854, as a fundamental doctrine of Christian-

ity. If the doctrine of Slavery extension is now implicitly held by our Church, what is to forbid its being,
in a few years, set forth in the creed?—I BELIEVE
IN THE EXTENSION OF SLAVERY. This
will be a better recommendation to protection and to
support, than "I believe in the Son of God," in the
section of country where I have been, on the Border.
This is the simple truth, and I can obtain, from slaveholders, testimony to its truth, over their own signa
tures!

In the abstract, Slavery is either a blessing or it is a
curse—it cannot be both, or a little of either. On this
issue, we in the Church will soon be compelled to choose
our sides. I have chosen mine—and who is there to
forbid me, while the creed remains as it is?

"Ah, we'll have a canon passed," I hear some
Southern Hotspur say, "to silence you gentlemen's
trumpets in the pulpits."

"But, oh, sir," I reply, "I will plead the canon of
the Gospel, and the creeds of the Church! There is
no security but an amendment to the creed—and then
I can be deposed for heresy!"

Let the Church be warned in time. Let the treatment
of Bishop Meade, in the Old Dominion, and the shame-
ful persecution of a poor missionary of the Church, on
the Border, warn us all that danger is at hand—yea,
laying its heavy hand upon us; the next step will be,
to sign and seal the death-warrant of our Religious
Liberty.

CHAPTER XXVIII.

DURING the winter of 1854, I made every effort possible, which my means and my circumstances permitted, to obtain a place of residence for my family, either at Leavenworth City or at Kickapoo. I made repeated applications to the keeper of the hotel at Leavenworth. He as often told me, that ladies could not be accommodated, on any terms. It was the same at Kickapoo. At one time, as I before related, I had made a contract for the old Indian Mission House; but, through the influence of the "Self-Defensives," a Methodist Parson had to violate, not only his word and honor, but a written contract was repudiated by him.

To render my situation more desperate, a letter from a brother clergyman, enclosing me sixty-three dollars, was robbed. My remittance check for half a year's salary, from the " Committee of the Church Missionary Society," was abstracted. I felt delicate to remind the Committee of what I supposed arose from its neglect, and I did not write to its secretary until months had passed. When I did write for information, I learned that my check had been duly forwarded, but that they could not exactly say to which office on the Border; but that it was either Weston or St. Joseph. I will refer to my search after this letter, in a following chapter.

8   [169]

Having no place actually where to go, in the Territory, I concluded that my wife must remain at Weston,
and that I must be separated from her, the greater part
of the time. I could get no place to preach at, in Leavenworth City. At the garrison chapel, there was no
admittance for me now. In days gone by, I was told,
" that, at any time I would consent to give them a service, the commanding officer would send a carriage for
me." But, now, Chaplain Kerr would insult me, by
occasionally asking me if the Reverend Mr. Irish, at St.
Joseph, could not be procured to preach for the church
people at the garrison. Here I was, on the spot, and
on the ground given me to cultivate, while the Reverend Mr. I. was absent forty miles by land, and one
hundred miles by water, and in a field of labor as dis-
tinct as could possibly be—he in Missouri, and under
the jurisdiction of the Bishop of Missouri.

At Kickapoo, I most frequently spent the Lord's
day. This was but three miles distant from Weston ;
I would walk the distance, and cross the river in John
Ellis' flat-boat, when the ice would permit. The river
does not often close before the first of January ; several times during the past ten or twelve years it has
remained open during the winter, though, under such
circumstances, the ice would be very troublesome,
coming down the stream in masses. It is always more
desirable to have the river frozen over, permitting foot
men and horse-teams to cross. I was thankful for the
natural bridge; it saved me time, and I did not have
any ferriage to pay.

Well, at Kickapoo City I was the first preacher.

This made the Methodists jealous—"an Episcopal clergyman the first among the bushes." This would never do. The old missionary—and a New Yorker too, at that—went round to inquire where he could purchase a " nigger " I did not want to purchase any " nigger." So the question between the preachers to gain the affections of the people, and to have the privilege of occupying the log-house on Sunday, was "nigger or no nigger." I was "no nigger," and I became "no preach." "No song, no supper."

I was now obliged to go to my much-persecuted friend, William Braham, and ask him to allow me to officiate at his house: this permission was given, and there to two or three I preached the Gospel; and before I left, I buried one of these. This William Braham was a discreet, good man; he was, by trade, a carpenter; he obtained work afterwards at Fort Leavenworth, and my last foothold at Kickapoo was gone.

At this crisis my expenses had been much greater than the sum which the Church had promised me. My outlay in reaching the Territory was nearly equal to half a year's salary, while at the end of the half-year, for reasons before stated, I had not received one dollar.

Something must be done. I did not wish to leave the Territory.

Early in March, 1855, I determined to go out on the prairie, erect me a log-hut, like my neighbors, and preach to those who might feel disposed to hear, in the open air during the coming season. Never after this time did I attempt to preach at Kickapoo or at
h

CHAPTER XXIX.

IN HUNGER AND COLD.

To quit Weston, Kickapoo, and Leavenworth I had been very long desirous; I felt that it would be madness to attempt to do so during the intense cold of mid-winter; but winter lingered this season in the lap of spring. When a bright and beautiful day appeared, I would say: "Lo, the winter is past, the rain is over and gone; the flowers appear on the earth; the time of the singing of birds is come, and the voice of the turtle is heard in our land." Allowing my imagination "to paint to-morrow like this day," I took my blanket, Indian and Border style, and determined to become a "Squatter Sovereign."

On this journey I had purposed travelling fourteen miles, three from Weston to Kickapoo, and eleven from this place to Penseneau's Crossing of the Stranger. The Stranger is a beautiful little stream, running very nearly south, through the eastern part of the Territory, and emptying into the Kansas river. The first choice claims were, of course, near the banks of the Missouri; but the second choice were on Stranger creek. At Penseneau's Crossing, they had purposed laying off a town by the name of Martinsburg. There were two or three numerous families of the Martins settled here, from Platte County. A young lawyer by the name of

Boyd, residing at Kickapoo, but originally from Tennessee, contemplated making a town of this, and doubtless would have accomplished it, had he not been so unfortunate as to have been appointed one of the Judges of Election, when Whitfield ran the first time for Congress. Boyd was from a Slave State, and I presume would have voted for Slavery in Kansas; but no official of Reeder's could be sound on the "goose." When the Missourians presented themselves to vote, Boyd insisted upon all swearing in their votes; this was enough. He had but one eye, but this they swore they would deprive him of. I took tea with the crowd at "Hays' Hotel," *i. e.*, the old log belonging to the Kickapoos—on the night after the election. Boyd's squeamish conscience came in for blessings in disguise. He was sitting then at the table, but taking it quite coolly.

Boyd, like the rest of the Real Estate brokers, had determined to make money out of Martinsburg; he got placards printed and posted up, telling us all, and the rest of the world, that there was no place like Martinsburg. I was not deceived by his statement into any such belief, and yet I thought that perhaps I had better go there and lay the foundation of the future city! I was obliged to go somewhere, and why not there? Not a blow had been struck, not a tree had been felled, not a stake had been driven; but there was the site of the city, and I might select the block which would hereafter become *relatively* the corner of Wall and Broadway! I went to Mr. A. G Boyd, and told him my plans. He was glad to see

me, gave me the first choice of the town, on conditions
that a log-church be·at once erected, and a log-dwell-
ing put up. I took his written agreement. It was, of
course, noïsed abroad that Boyd's fortune was made,
the Episcopal Bishop—as some of the ignorant ones
used to call me—had selected Martinsburg as his future
See! Fortunes ahead, now, was the word! But not
so fast. On almost every placard advertising Martinsburg, which had the name of A. G. Boyd signed
to it, had also affixed thereto an interpolation not furnished to the printer—"Abolitionist" was written as
an exponent of the character of A. G. Boyd; because
A. G. Boyd had given me, as a clergyman of the Episcopal church, a block of wild, unimproved land, twelve
miles removed from the Missouri. Martinsburg stock,
after this, could not be given away—bankruptcy was
now evident. They could have endured the cholera,
or the yellow fever, or the small-pox, but the Episcopal preacher had gone there, that was enough. "Boyd
was undoubtedly an Abolitionist." His little coop,
which he called his Law Office, in Kickapoo City, was
burned, and he was obliged to leave!

Well, I had taken my blanket and was now on my
way, early in March, to take a look at my property.
I did not take a horse;. I expected to be gone two or
three days, and I could not afford to keep a horse this
length of time, nor feed him if I had taken him; nor was
there the least certainty that I would bring him back with
me, for I have frequently found the poor Indians looking
all over the country for their little ponies, which had
been stolen from them by the highly-civilized whites!

After I had travelled about six miles, not meeting in that distance a human being, I sat down at a spring, took from my pocket a couple of biscuit, which I had sliced, and a little piece of ham inserted, *à la* sandwich. This I ate, and then turned me down on "all-fours," forming a natural hydraulic machine, and thus slaked my thirst. I felt refreshed, and taking out an apple I went on my way, munching it.

I passed many *foundations.* Perhaps I had better explain. Four logs laid in a quadrangle constituted a pre-emption claim of a "Squatter Sovereign." This was an indication that a building was in the *course* of erection. A shingle would very generally be set with one end driven into the ground, and on the other would be found written the name of the architect, and the proprietor. If you loved peace, why then you would not think of squatting within half a mile of this foundation, on either side; but if you should admire the taste of the absent architect, and fancy his location, why the first ox-team that you could hire you might bring and sprawl the four logs all over; and then draw four logs yourself, place them some little distance from the place where the others were laid, place the shingle as aforesaid, with your own name written thereon, as architect and proprietor, with the additional caution— "If I find any d——d rascal touching this foundation, I will cut his liver out!"

Travel on, it is getting very cold. Blanket in requisition; four more miles to travel. I expect to stay at Azariah Martin's—reach Azariah's log hut, but he is not there. The morning was pleasant, and I suppose they took their horses and have gone off fifteen or twenty miles to·spend the day! Very social people in a new country. However, it was evident that they did not expect any call while they were absent, as a plow-chain and a padlock fastened the home-made door. I could have got in through several places, between the logs, but I would have been but precious little less exposed to the cold, and my landscape view would have been cut off. · Hungry, wearied and very cold, with night coming on. Cannot be helped. There is no snow on the ground, just get out of the wind and sit down and rest yourself. The next time, go out and tell Azariah Martin when you are coming! "Miserable comforters are ye all," said Job. I think Job would have turned comforter to me himself, that night in Kansas. Fortune was still *ahead!*

A rather frightful thought now occurred to me. There is no lack of wolves in Kansas! Here was I, a shepherd, indeed, but having neither gun nor dog. A place of refuge I must have in reserve, should the prairie wolves begin to bark in any great number. I tride to insert my head between one or two of the most glaring of Azariah's "oak openings," but my head was larger than I had at first imagined it to be—the logs were as inhospitable as the plow-chain; they said, decidedly, "no admittance."

But poverty is the mother of invention. The log was low and the chimney was lower, and nearly as wide as the house itself; to the initiated this would need no explanation, but it is barely possible that this book may fall into the hands of some Fifth Avenue

Belle, and I will attempt an explanation. "One-half of the world knows not how the other half lives."

We have in contemplation the erection of a log cabin for the particular information of the Fifth Avenue lady of fashion. The cabin shall be sixteen feet in the clear—quite a large cabin for mere squatting purposes. Well, if the cabin is to be sixteen feet each way inside, we must have logs cut full eighteen feet long, to allow of saddling and notching—*i. e.*, the end of one log must be chopped off in shape like the back-bone of a rather poor horse, and this is called saddling; that is, this is prepared to receive the notch, which is made by chopping the end of another log into a shape such as a saddle presents in the under part, where the padding is. Saddle and notch—notch and saddle away now, at the end, and on the end of every log, until your house is up.

Well, now you take a look to see where you would like to have the ornamentals, as, for instance, the chimney. Ah, very well; we get a large cross-cut saw now, and saw out about eight feet in length of about five of the logs. So the logs are cut out, and of course a horse and cart could be backed into the cabin. A small cabin now, about six or eight feet square, must be built around this hole for the egress of the smoke, which may be made in the cabin fire-place. This additional cabin is not, at first, built up its entire length, neither is it raised often above the gable end of the cabin. Oh, well, I can tell you better than this. You have seen towers to churches, built up in *part* and roofed over, until such times as the trustees can secure cash

8*

enough to surmount it with a spire? Very well, then; the backwoodsman has frequently to leave his chimney in this condition, either from want of help, or want of money, or want of disposition; it was from the latter want that Azariah's chimney was not completed. He never did complete it. He said that the smoke was much lighter than the logs, and he hoped that it would always have an inclination to ascend, and thereby save him any further trouble.

If the castle-building ladies of the Fifth Avenue cannot understand the foregoing mode of construction, then let them ask John C. Fremont, he can tell them all about it.

If this little book should become a classic, then the boys will confound the construction of my cabin as much as the boys I once knew, did Cæsar's bridge.

The wolves did bark! I barked up the logs and I barked down the chimney! I made up a fire, but I could not make up any bread—there was neither meal, flour, nor bacon. When these failed Azariah, as they very frequently did, then he would go on a visiting and a borrowing tour. There was every evidence that he had been expelled from the cabin on this day or the day before, by his craving creditor—appetite.

Dinnerless, supperless, and a glorious prospect for breakfastless, I laid me down, and pulled the blanket over me.

I know a Rector not many miles from New York, who will say, if he ever reads this—"Screw loose," "screw loose, somewhere!" Yet this Rector can afford to get "bread and butter," and I can and will write about "when I could get none."

CHAPTER XXX.

ON the 13th day of March, 1855, several relatives arrived at Weston, on the first boat which came up the river. I mentioned to these my condition, and proposed that we should prepare to go out into the Territory and camp until we could build a cabin.

This was agreed to. I purchased forty yards of common cotton cloth for the making of a tent. Twenty yards of rag carpet to spread on the ground for our bed, and two or three pairs of common blankets. All our bedding and clothing, save the few articles we wore daily, had been lost. In addition to these necessary articles to protect us in some degree from the cold, we procured some flour, and meal, and bacon, with a little tea, sugar, and coffee, as very great luxuries.

Our articles for cooking consisted of a tin tea-pot and a tin coffee-pot, a frying pan, an iron oven or pot to bake our bread; a tin bucket, a tin dish or pan, for mixing our bread, a few tin cups, and tin platters. Knives and forks and spoons we dispensed with, except as far as we could supply the deficiency by our own whittling knives. In addition to these, we procured a couple of the Squatter Sovereigns' "*vade mecum*" axes.

The next morning we procured our team to take us

fourteen miles, charge six dollars, and two dollars to John Ellis for ferriage.

We started and got out beyond Kickapoo. My companions had not seen as much of the unappropriated domain of Uncle Sam as I had, and, of course, I had to answer all questions with reference thereto. The "*foundations*," and the "*cautions*," afforded some merriment, and also led to a profound discussion of "Squatter Law." When I had got through with my exposition, the general impression among the company was, that they had never been in a free country before! "Very possible," as Mr. Barnacle would have said.

We kept on the great military road until we came to Mr. Fortune's log tavern. Mr. F. had laid off a city, about a mile from the city of Martinsburg, and had named it "Mount Pleasant." For once, my usual caution and extreme prudence failed me; I inquired, "Where a wagon route might be found down to the city of Martinsburg?" The old man looked through his specs, but he did not open his lips. He wished the city of Martinsburg to remain without inhabitants! We drove along through the timber in the direction of the city of our refuge. It had been snowing very much during the past hour or two, and it continued on all that afternoon. We soon approached a point from whence we could have seen Martinsburg, were it not snowing at the time. We stood on the high bluff which overhangs "Stranger Creek." A dead halt now. We had approached the point where, if any man or horse designed to go to the Creek, he must descend. We took the horses out of the wagon, and led them down the precipice, certainly quite one hundred and fifty feet from the summit to the bottom. We fastened the horses below. and returned to take out our provisions, and carry them down. The wagon was now to be got down. We fastened one of the wheels, one or two of us took hold of the tongue, and one or two grasped each a wheel, and all were charged to hold back with all their might, as our lives depended upon the issue of that wagon down that hill! A tremendous rattling and shouting, on our part, as we descended, brought out Azariah Martin!

Azariah was smoking a pipe made of corn-cob, such as old General Jackson had used and pronounced "Nonpareil."

We asked Azariah whether we could get some dinner at his cabin? He said "that they were all sick with the chills."

We loaded up our team again, put the horses to, and drove along about three-quarters of a mile further, to the place we had selected for our camping-ground, in the near vicinity of wood and water.

The first thing in great requisition was a fire, and such a fire as, should it snow for a week, could not be quenched! The axes were put in play, and about five cords of wood, consisting of the bodies and limbs of trees, were heaped up; some brushwood, and leaves, and paper were lighted, and a fire that was a fire, soon blazed.

Now for tent-making. Two stakes were procured about eight feet in length, with a crotch or fork in one end of each, the other end of each was sharpened and driven into the ground, putting the two stakes on a line with each other (as I believe you cannot very well place them otherwise), ten feet apart. We now cut a ten-foot pole, for a ridge, and laid it in the two crotches of the two upright stakes. We now got out our cotton cloth, which had not been at all prepared for a tent, and arranged it over these timbers in a manner such as would have suggested itself to the merest tyro in tent-making. We spread the rag carpet on the ground inside of the tent. Took our provisions from the wagon, and placed them in the tent. The poor horses were taken out and tied for the night: they began to eat the bark from the limbs of the trees; I insisted upon some of our corn-meal being given to the horses; it cost a dollar and a half a bushel, and murmurs were made at the proposition, but the horses got a little of the meal.

As our cooking utensils were in a state of untidiness, and ourselves tired and wet, we thought it best to send a committee to inquire if Mrs. Martin would not bake us a loaf of bread. She consented, and charged us eighty cents for baking the loaf. We kept cool, but intended to be our own bakers henceforth. The bacon was fried, and the tea was made, and we sat down on the stumps of the trees to enjoy

"Life by the prairie fire."

Azariah Martin came up to take tea with us, and to see how we liked the bread!

We sat up by the fire that night until after twelve

o'clock. It was quite cold. It had stopped snowing. We turned into the tent; divided the blankets between each other. We each took our turn of getting up to warm ourselves at the fire, during the night. One of the party had his hat blown off the limb of a tree, into the fire, and entirely consumed, as we supposed, for it was never heard from after that night—it was a new hat. Another of the party had a hole burnt in his velvet cap while it was on his head, by a spark, we must believe—the hole was quite extensive; but a cap with an opening in both ends was just as good in Kansas, as one with only the necessary enlargement for the head! I do not think that the person has re- newed his cap to this day.

The morning came, and we had our breakfast; I left to take the wagon back to Weston, intending to walk on my return to the camp.

I stayed in Weston a day or two, and then set out on foot for the tent on Stranger Creek. When I arrived, the camp was in a state of mutiny! The novelty had worn off, and home in New Jersey and New York, was lauded to the skies. They all began to tell me their experience in prospecting. One had purchased a claim for ten dollars, from an Indian, but a white man " umped" it the next day. The rest had seen nothing that pleased them.

Sickness, poverty and starvation, they found in every cabin which they had visited. I cheered up the party, and told them to wait until better weather set in, and until we should get a claim, and have a cabin to protect us from the cold.

While I sat there comforting the party, a man came to the camp to ask us if we would not go over to his cabin, about a mile and a half distant, and help him to "raise up" two Mustang ponies, which were pretty nearly dead with hunger! We went over; one of the ponies died. In the cabin of the man there was death. My brother, though a layman, had buried an infant the day before this, and the mother of that infant was there lying at the point of death. She had been salivated to a most cruel degree. I attended her for days. I think that she died at peace with God, and in a full hope of pardon through Christ. She was buried by me a few yards from her cabin. I took this opportunity to tell the people who I was, and that I would preach regularly in the neighborhood.

We remained in tent about two weeks; I did not see that anybody was likely to take any interest in the building up of Martinsburg, so I let the idea of settlement on the site of the town vanish from my thoughts. A cabin and a claim must be purchased. A cabin and a claim is the subject of the next chapter.

CHAPTER XXXI.

THE woman whom I consoled in her last hour, as mentioned in the previous chapter, and buried near the cabin in which she died, left a cabin and a claim behind her. The preëmption law does not permit any "willing away" a claim. Mrs. J. had been a widow, or worse than a widow, her husband had deserted her. She had now left behind her a married daughter, who was poor. According to Squatter Law, any of our party could have taken the cabin and the claim, without giving any consideration. Our party had a consultation, and we proposed to buy the claim. But before we had well made up our minds, the son-in-law of the late Mrs. J. came to inquire if we did not wish to buy the cabin and the claim. We gave him his price, and possession was taken.

The quality of the rudeness of this cabin must be placed in the superlative degree. It was 12 feet square, the walls were about 8 feet high, mud chimney, five thousand air holes, but no window; it had a ground or prairie floor. It was, when we bought it, used as a stable. We were obliged to shovel out a load or two of material, which a New Englander would like to have had to enrich his garden, but which was considered useless in Kansas. The countenances of the party brightened up considerably on the signing of the "quit-claim deed," which made this important residence our own, to have and to hold, and to squat in, to our hearts' content. This cabin was a mile and a half from our camping ground, and there was no way of reaching it with a team, even if we had had one, without making a circuit of six miles. It was resolved that we should strike our tent, and carry up all the articles on our shoulders. It was a very difficult job. It occupied all of that day and the next to get our truck up to the cabin. I longed for some pastiles, or a little frankincense, or a large quantity of cologne, to regale the apartments, but we could not even procure a piece of lime. Ammonium, they say, is healthy; with this hope, we inhaled it in large quantities.

The horses had left behind them some prairie hay. We procured part of it, and spread it down one side of the cabin, and laid the carpet down over the hay, thus making preparations for our repose. We never were more wearied in our lives than we were this night. But we had yet to prepare supper. Water was now distant from our cabin three-quarters of a mile. Whoever should volunteer to go for the water now, must walk one mile and a half. Well, one must cut the wood, another must do the cooking, and a third must go after the water. Thus matters were arranged. The frying of the bacon, I was gratified to perceive, had some qualifying effect on the common atmosphere of the room.

The next morning we did as we had done the night

previous. It was corn-meal bread and bacon for breakfast, bacon and corn-meal bread for dinner, with a little of the gravy for a relish; and at supper-time we varied, and returned to corn-meal bread and bacon. If Professor Pierce of Harvard could only have given us a recipe how to use these twenty-one times a week, and yet never have them all on the table at the same time, he would have conferred a lasting blessing on humanity!

We were informed by the gentleman from whom we had purchased our estate, that there were about four hundred fence-rails scattered all over the supposed 160 acres, which would fall to our share. We went out to look at these, and the other appurtenances of the claim. We came to the conclusion that there was very little more wanting to make the claim a capital farm than what is wanting on every other farm, as it comes first from the hands of "Uncle Sam." It required a good deal of money, and a lifetime of hard labor, for the strongest of men, aided by the strongest of the domestic animals, such as the ox and the horse.

These 160 acres which we had claimed and paid for, would have more than kept us all busy to get a livelihood from; but of course every man wanted a "cabin and a claim." It took two or three weeks for the rest of our party to make up their minds; but by the end of that time they had done so. It was now all hurry and bustle to get the foundation logs cut and laid, and the "shingles," with the names of the proposed builders, and the time when the claim was made, marked thereon.

Two or three incidents occurred while about this important work, which may not be uninteresting. At one claim, one of our party had just got his logs down and his shingle set up, according to law, when an ox-team was seen slowly plodding along from a grove of timber towards the point at which we stood on the prairie. We soon discovered that the oxen had logs in tow, and that, in all probability, the men who were driving the oxen were architects. They approached us. It had been their design to lay a foundation very near the spot where we stood; but they observed that we "had been and got ahead of them, and that we might have their logs." We thanked them very kindly, and took their logs, which they had been all day getting out, and laid them as the second tier on our house.

They wanted to know which one of us was the preacher, and at whose cabin the preaching would be next Sunday. We satisfied them in these particulars. They were very anxious that we should not confine our preaching to any particular locality. They thought that the better way would be to bring it right home to their doors.

The other incident which I referred to as occurring during the location of claims, I will relate, just to show how the system works.

We observed a young man one forenoon, with an axe in his hand, stepping off, as we were satisfied, a claim that he was making. He seemed to be in much doubt about the result of his measurement. He stepped it off once or twice more, and then went to chop down his logs for a "foundation." We went to him and told him that there was not room for a claim between that which one of our party had made and that which he felt disposed to appropriate to himself. He became furious, and was all for fight. The altercation, and the stepping, and the measuring, occupied the whole afternoon. Finally he left, under a protest, and with a declaration that he would be back next morning with a party of friends to settle the question. The general impression was, that there would be warm, if not bloody work, the next day; and to prevent anything of this kind, I proposed that a compass should be taken, and a tape-line, having chains marked on it, should be taken, and the ground measured carefully, and if there was the possibility of a chance for a claim, to let the man have it. There was a disposition to measure the ground, but pretty little to give the absent man a claim. We measured the ground, and found that he could not get a claim.

The next morning both parties assembled. The stranger had brought two men with him. All came prepared to defend their rights. It was decided to leave the matter to the arbitration of three individuals, each party choosing one, and these two selecting the third. The compass and the line were placed in the hands of the umpires, and the like result as we had arrived at before, was declared by them, viz., that there was " not room." The powder of- both parties was saved. We all parted, wishing each other success in cabining and in claiming.

CHAPTER XXXII.

PREACHING THE GOSPEL, AND FINDING ONE'S SELF.

THE time embraced in this chapter of events, I would like to have understood as the spring and summer of 1855. The expenses of my family had been very considerable, and, as I had not received any aid whatever from the authorities in the Church, as an honest man I was under obligations to attempt something, as a means of livelihood.

I will first state our mode of conducting services, out on the Stranger.

There was good land on both sides of this creek, consequently, there were cabins on both sides, and people dwelling in them. The creek could not always be forded by women and children, so I proposed to preach at Penseneau's Crossing to the congregations assembled on either side of the creek. I never used any service but that furnished by the Prayer Book; but to attempt to have used the service, as conducted in Trinity Church, New York, for instance, would have been supremely ridiculous. While I officiated in this neighborhood, I had two or three funerals to attend. I have described a wedding—let me draw a picture of a funeral, on the Border.

Mrs. M. had been the mother of a numerous family

of sons and daughters—the most of whom lived at home, or in the neighborhood.

The body of the mother was to be consigned to the grave. The neighbors, as a matter of course, would all be there. One turned his oxen out to graze, and, in his rough plowman's garb, went to attend the funeral; another laid his axe down, and went to help to dig the grave; one of the sons of the deceased came over to a friend's, to borrow a cart, which was to be used as a hearse; another, who could handle a plane, went to help to make the coffin for his own mother. The husband of the deceased would not ask me to officiate, as none of the family belonged to the Church; a friend came, and told me the circumstances. What could I say in the premises, but that I would attend the funeral? I went over to the log cabin, distant about a mile and a half, and helped to place the body in the coffin; the wagon, having a pair of very young and unbroken oxen before it, was drawn up to the door. The nigh ox had a rope tied about its head, to lead it by. A son of the deceased led the team along, after the coffin had been laid in the wagon. I followed behind the wagon, to the grave; but the great majority went in directions by which they could get more easily to the grave. As the ox-team, lead by one of the chief mourners, and myself, were pursuing our journey over a very uneven road, we discovered many persons gathering towards the burial-spot, on horseback, in wagons, and on foot. They were collecting from miles around.

The solemn Burial Service made a deep impression upon that sturdy pioneer throng. The reader may rest satisfied that I did not let that opportunity pass, without endeavoring to lead the hearts of that rude assembly to acknowledge Christ as the "Resurrection and the Life."

At this funeral, plans were devised for more stated services. A grove, in a central position, was selected, where seats should be constructed for the accommodation of the people. This was done by cutting down a number of trees, and, when the limbs had been chopped off, split into halves, and these halves smoothed off with axes, and then placed in the manner of benches. A dry goods box was placed between the bodies of two standing trees, as a platform, or a pulpit, for myself; and overhead, between the two standing trees, brushwood was arranged, to protect me from the sun. Here we had Methodist singing and Episcopal preaching.

After we had progressed thus far, the weather had become quite pleasant. My wife was still at Weston —she now desired to come over with her infant child, and share our miseries. If we were to have ladies and children in the cabin, it must be fitted up a little. We got a dry-goods box for a table; we extemporized a bedstead, by boring auger-holes in the logs of the cabin-wall, and inserting poles therein, and propping up the other ends, by stakes driven into the floor; and then laying slats, split out of oak trees, à la cabinet bedstead. We kept adding to our comforts, of course; but this was the beginning of housekeeping on the Prairie. All our housekeeping articles, as before stated, had been lost on the Missouri. My wife and child were brought over in the middle of May. She and her sister-in-law amused themselves killing rattlesnakes, as long as the novelty lasted.

Our party bought, between us, a couple of yoke of oxen, two cows, a horse, wagon, plow, and other farming utensils. We got a Missouri settler to come and break up our garden, with our help. We fenced the garden, and put in the crop. In addition to what the garden would produce, we must have some corn for the cattle, during the coming winter. We had no land broken, neither could we break it; we formed a partnership with the Missourian, who had broken the garden. We united teams with him, and went to work on his land—for the fencing of which he had rails already split. There we prepared the land for about thirty-five acres of corn-land, and chopped in the seed with an axe. In addition to this, we aided each other in the erection of four cabins, during the summer. All the firewood which we needed, I was obliged to cut out of the forest. Every drop of water which we used, if for ordinary purposes, I had to go and yoke up the oxen, and take a barrel three-quarters of a mile for it—if for drinking, then I had to take the horse, fasten a two-gallon jug to the saddle, and drive the same distance. If the most ordinary article should be wanted, then the same horse must be mounted, and driven fifteen miles for it, and fifteen miles back—always costing four times as much to reach the article, as it was worth at the store. Very frequently, indeed, did I go this distance for a bushel of corn-meal; and when the corn-meal was reached, so precious was the commodity, that many competitors would endeavor to outbid each other, to gain it.

This state of things continued for the whole summer, as a matter of course.

In the meantime we preached regularly, every Sunday, in the grove. On one occasion there was a negro man by the name of Joe, who was lying down in the grass, at some little distance from the "white folks," listening to me preaching. Joe kept grinning all the while, as if there was something supremely ridiculous in my remarks. I was myself conscious that unusual solemnity possessed me, and that I was quite energetic in my gestures. I went to Joe, immediately after service, and asked him what he had been grinning at? Joe laughed now immoderately. I will explain. The brush-wood, which screened me from the sun, shelved off behind me, like a shed. Joe anticipated that I would cap the climax, by knocking my head vigorously against the fixtures.

CHAPTER XXXIII.

THINGS progress quite rapidly in a new country, although the highest attainments would be considered very ordinary displays by a New Yorker. For instance, during this summer of '55, I had preached at the crossing of a Creek, where the people either stood or sat down, or did both by turns; from this we had progressed to a grove where they had hewn log seats; it was now in contemplation to erect a " log cabin," to be public property! This was designed, according to the liberal wishes of the masses, to be a School-house for all on week days, and a preaching-house for everybody on Sundays. About fifteen heads of families felt disposed to enter into this project. A meeting was called, to assemble near a certain spring on a certain day. I was asked to draw up a " Constitution" for the Society, to be submitted to the " Sovereigns" at the meeting. For the next week or two I received ten or twelve calls from persons desirous to know where this building was to be located? Some two or three of these persons had come from a distance of seven miles. The movement was regarded as highly important. The most thought that there was a speculation at the bottom of the project. It was regarded as the beginning of a town, perhaps a city. I was not in the secret if this was the design, and yet I saw that the movement did require a little watching.

There were Free. State men and Pro-Slavery men equally interested, and in about equal numbers. I began to be a little suspicious that power might be the object sought for in this matter. Trustees, and other officers, were to be appointed for this joint School, or Meeting-house. I disclosed my views to a few on whom I could rely, and told them how to conduct themselves in case the Pro-Slavery party should muster too strongly at the meeting. I was afraid that if everything fell into the hands of the Pro-Slavery men, then, even after we had built the cabin, I should be forbidden to preach in it.

We assembled on the day appointed at the spring. There were about fifteen men. I observed with much satisfaction, that the Free State men were the most numerous.

For two or three hours we debated the size and the material of which that one-room building should be— sixteen feet square was decided as the size. Each one was to have cut and hewn on his own place, three logs, and have them drawn to the spot hereafter to be described. In addition to this, each was to give in money two dollars and fifty cents, to procure a door, and windows, and flooring, and also for the plastering of the room.

After this was done I read the "Constitution ;" which was debated and altered in many particulars. I found I had a thousand things to learn with reference to backwoods school-keeping. The permanent officers had now to be appointed, and I gave the private signal which had been agreed upon in caucus of the Free State men. Nomination after nomination was made by the Free State party of those Pro-Slavery men whom we knew could neither *read* nor *write ;* these were generous enough to decline the honors, and return the compliment by nominating Free State men who could read and write. With much show of humility these accepted the offices. It was with the greatest difficulty that I could preserve my gravity at the complete success of this manœuvre. A Free State Treasurer was appointed, who received the moneys on the spot. A building committee was appointed, a majority of whom were Free State men. The Trustees were quite closely balanced, but in a full meeting the Free State interest, on any important issue, would have been sustained.

The site was chosen, and the logs were drawn on the ground ; but when I was taken severely ill the interest was lost in the project, and I never had the privilege to preach within the walls of the building, which furnished us with so much matter for discussion in its inception.

CHAPTER XXXIV.

ONCE MORE CALLED TO MOURN.

WHILE struggling along, working a mile or two from the cabin in the field, or endeavoring to make things a little smooth for my wife at home, our second and only child of five months old, whom I had named after one who had been more than a mother to me in my struggles with poverty in my boyhood, very suddenly died. It was a sweet child. It would lie on the poor couch and laugh at the sunbeams pouring in through the many holes of our cabin; and the mother would laugh at it as the loveliest sunbeam of all.

My brothers went and dug another little grave. A very pretty little walnut coffin was made; many a kind-hearted person came to attend the funeral: my wife was so unwell she could not sit up on the bed. I was very feeble, but I read a portion of the service at the cabin. A neighbor took the coffin under his arm, I was placed on horseback, and we wended our sad way to the grave, and there I read, for the second time, the service over my own child. A parent's only earthly comfort, and a mother's little companion in her loneliness, in that home worse than exile, was buried from our sight. The mother was never able to go and look on that little grave. When I got sufficiently well, a week or two before I left the country, I went and had the body of our first babe raised out of the grave at Weston, and took it over to the Territory, and buried it in the same grave with the last, in a beautiful grove on the top of what the Indians call Strawberry Hill, from the circumstance that vast numbers of this fruit grow wild thereon.

Lovely in their lives were these infants, and in death they are not divided.

CHAPTER XXXV.

TEN DISMAL AND ANXIOUS WEEKS.

DURING the months of August and September, great quantities of rain fell in Kansas. The cabins of all the settlers were almost constantly in a state of flood. "Fever and Ague" laid both my wife and myself very low. All those to whom we could look for aid were likewise sick. We were reduced to mere skeletons, prostrated, without the least energy. No medicines which we could procure would keep off the disease for more than two or three days at a time. My brother, himself quite unwell, often rode into the State of Missouri for medicines, but they effected no service.

In this condition I started out on the journey to look for my remittance from the Committee in New York. Nearly a year had now elapsed, and I had never received my salary. I was in very great need. On a day when I did not expect to have a chill, I started on a journey of thirty miles, on horseback, to inquire about the letter which the Secretary of the Domestic Committee had written to me had been forwarded in due time.

I had not ridden more than two or three miles, before I was very conscious that I would have a severe chill in an hour or so. I rode on, and when I reached

[200

Atchison, on the Missouri river, it came on. I crossed the ferry, got a man to help me into the saddle, and on I went for fifteen miles further, with a very high fever on, and a pain in my head and back almost beyond endurance. Just at evening I reached a cabin about eight miles below St. Joseph; I stopped at it. The inmates discovered, without my telling them, what the difficulty was. They made a pallet for me on the floor, and prepared a dish of strong coffee; after I had rested and drank the coffee, I felt much better. I had my horse brought out, and started once more, and reached St. Joseph about eight o'clock. I did not stop in the town, but went out into the country three miles, to the house of a very dear friend, Mrs. James Cargill. This family was from Wheeling, Va. They were slaveholders. I had lived with them for fifteen months. Mrs. C. was a communicant of the church. The family knew my sentiments well, but they also knew that I was not a disturber.

When I drew up at the door on this evening, I had not seen Mrs. C. for two years previous. I need not say that our meeting was a joyful one, indeed it was most affectionate. Mrs. C. had a large family of children and grand-children. I was treated with the greatest respect by them all. They were all decided Pro-Slavery people, but they never said I was wrong in disapproving of the outrages in Kansas. I would not stay longer than that night with Mrs. C. When I was about leaving, in the morning, she loaded me down with delicacies for my wife, and would not let me leave until I had faithfully promised to fetch my wife over to her
9*

house and stay a month or months, to recruit her health.
I promised to do this, and rode away.   When I reached
town I went directly to the post-office, nothing doubt-
ing but that my letter, with a check for my salary,
would be there—but it was not.   It was too late in the
day now to permit of my reaching home that night, so
I stayed all day in St. Joseph with a married daughter
of Mrs. C., and about sundown I started, with the in-
tention of staying at the log house of my friend of the
previous evening.   I reached it about nine o'clock, but
the whole night I never slept—the musquitoes were
perfectly awful.   These people were Missourians, but
Free State in sentiment, and were almost decided to
go over into Kansas to live, with the hope that it would
become a Free State.

The next day I reached home, with a sad heart,
although I had some delicacies for my wife, which
money could not have procured in that country.

I rested at home a day or two, and then started
again for Kickapoo, Weston, and Fort Leavenworth,
in search of my letter—this was a journey back and
forth of fifty miles—it took me two days.   I found no
letter.

I wrote now from Fort Leavenworth to New York,
and told the Secretary that the letter had undoubtedly
been robbed, as a previous one had been, with loss,
and begged that a duplicate might be forwarded, drawn
up after a form which I suggested, and to be sent to a
certain post-office; this I received by return of mail,
and also a letter from my Bishop, containing a loan
from his own private funds.   I returned this, with

many thanks, at once. In the same letter from the Bishop, I was advised to retire from the Territory. I was glad of the relief. I wrote to the Committee, resigning my mission, to take effect on the 1st day of November, 1855.

I got my check cashed, paid a number of debts, and prepared to leave the Territory.

CHAPTER XXXVI.

FAREWELL TO THE TERRITORY.

IT was very evident that the health of my wife and my own was failing very rapidly. For the three or four days previous to our journey to Missouri, to visit our friend Mrs. C., we could not help ourselves in the smallest matter. The Joe, before mentioned, was sent by his master several times a day to see what could be done for us.

While I lay in this critical state, a Committee of Squatters, Missourians too, came to inquire if I would not promise to go as a delegate to the Big Spring Convention, which was to select men to draw up the Topeka Constitution! Poor fellows, I told them that the very fact of a clergyman representing them would prejudice their cause. I did not wish to discourage them by saying that I took no interest in political matters, and that I would on no consideration think it my duty to meet at that Convention for the purpose desired. Had I been able to go, and had I gone, our neighborhood would have been pillaged, and probably we would have been murdered. As it was, the "Squatter Sovereign," published at Atchison, threatened our neighborhood in the following terms. "There is a nest of traitors a few miles west of this place, who will find themselves hanging from the limbs of the trees which overhang the Stranger, if they do not keep very quiet." I would not have gone to the Convention on any consideration; I was in the employ of the Church, and it sent me to do no such work, however praiseworthy in itself. I scrupulously kept away from all exciting meetings during my stay in the Territory; I challenge proof to the contrary.

The day arrived when we were not to leave, but to be taken out of the cabin. The farm wagon was driven to the door; our trunks were put in, and my wife and myself taken and laid on blankets in the bottom of the wagon. We left cabin and claim, furniture, &c., just as they were, and have never looked after them since. " All that a man hath will he give for his life " The wagon was driven about a mile, when we came to a soft piece of road, and the horses stopped, unable to draw the wagon. My brother, who was driving, left us and went in search of help; he returned with two or three men. The trunks were taken out of the wagon, my wife and myself were lifted out and laid on the top of the trunks. The wagon was then driven about one hundred yards on to the more compact earth, and ourselves and the trunks put back again into the wagon. In this way we were driven to Atchison, to take a boat up to St. Joseph. When we reached Atchison, I was carried to the hotel, the wagon could not be driven to the door. When we reached the hotel, I observed a number of the chivalry. The editors of the "Squatter Sovereign," J. H. Stringfellow, Bob Kelly, and —— Cundiff, looked daggers at me. I did not know but that the fate of the Rev. Pardee Butler awaited me. This was the place, and these were some of the gentlemen to which and to whom the honor belongs of sending down the Missouri, tied to a log, the above-named gentleman, who, I believe, is a Kentuckian by birth.

At first we were told that we could receive no room at the hotel. I did not know what to think of this at first, but I afterwards learned that there was not room. But I found there Mr. Peter T. Abell and his lady, from Weston. They were quite civil to us. We were allowed to sit in their room until one should be vacated in the house. P. T. A. was a decided Pro-Slavery man; he was a leader among the "Self-Defensives." He was the partner of the Law firm, "Abell & Stringfellow," of Weston. Mr. Abell had some *cause* if not *reason* to justify his decided opposition to Free State settlers. A negro man had run away from him, and this negro would occasionally write from Canada, very insulting letters to him.

While at Atchison we received no abuse; all the attention, however, which I had shown me here, where I was well known, I had to pay well for. For three days and nights I remained at A., insensible, as I am informed, the greater portion of the time. The steamer Edinburgh, however, came up in the middle of the third night after our arrival, when I was supported on the one side by a wife, herself sick, and the keeper of the hotel on the other, down to the steamer. After the steamer had left the levee on her way to St. Joseph, about forty miles distant, while I was sitting in the cabin, as I am informed, I fell down on the floor in a congestive chill which is considered in that country almost invariably fatal. I was carried to the state-room, and here, I learned afterwards, two gentlemen acquainted with the nature of the disease, did all which reason and experience suggested to them. I recovered, in some measure, my senses before we reached St. Joseph. When we reached the levee there, the Rev. Mr. Irish came on board. He approached me, and said, " Although I think you have done me a great wrong, I cannot withhold my sympathies from you in this condition." I did not understand him. I asked him to get me a carriage, that I might be taken out to my old friend, Mrs. Cargill's, three miles in the country. This I was told would be madness in my condition; the carriage was procured, and the Rev. Mr. I. had me taken to his own house, where I remained about ten days in a very critical state, attended by the best medical aid in the town, and by the most assiduous nursing care of Mr. I. and his family. It was the general opinion that I could not live. Mr. J. Cargill and his family visited me daily. When it was quite safe for me to be taken to the country, I was carried out to Mrs. C.'s, where two children could not have received as much fond attention as my wife and myself did for the period of one month. After I had left this region of country, I wrote letters of thanks for kindness received at the hands of Mr. I. and my dear friend, Mrs. C. It gives me pleasure now to do so, in a more public manner. On the 29th of October, 1855, we took the Polar Star, at St. Joseph, for St. Louis. It was on this trip down that Mr. J. W. Whitfield furnished me with the matter contained in a previous cha ter. He was then on his a t ashington.

CHAPTER XXXVII.

THE PAST AND THE PRESENT CONDITION OF KANSAS.

I HAVE thought that perhaps my view of the past and the present state of things in the Territory, would not be unacceptable, or altogether without utility.

I am very much amazed at the incredulity which seems to possess the minds of many very excellent men with reference to the outrages in Kansas.

They read of these deeds of demons in the newspapers, and the paper is thrown aside, with a sneer of utter scorn at the temerity of an editor who is so lost to a sense of truth as to insert such articles in his journal. And these persons are confirmed in their sentiments by two or three of the sober and conservative journals of New York, and the religious press very generally. The nearest approach to pandemonium that the editors of these journals have ever made in their lives, has been when they took a holiday at Saratoga or at Newport; therefore, they are not, neither can they be, with their present limited ideas of human nature, judges of affairs on the Border. Their opinion, I say, is worse than useless; they write of matters concerning which they show perfect ignorance. It would be infinitely better for humanity that they

[208]

should keep altogether silent; and say, "as we have no correspondents in that region of country, we have no reports which we regard as reliable" But instead of doing this, they sneer at the statements made in papers much better furnished with facts than they are themselves. While they caution their sober and grave readers to give no credence to the reports furnished to the journals which have the largest circulation among the people, they unconsciously become the *deceivers* of good men, and the aiders and abettors of criminals of the deepest dye. · This is an awful Responsibility for the Editors of these Journals to assume. I know readers of these papers in the City of New York, who are told by them every day that the reports from Kansas are fabrications, who if they could but be transported to Kansas for a day, they would fall down and weep over the outrages committed in the land of a Washington!

I have no interest in what I write, save that justice may not be driven from her throne; I trust that my experience will have some influence in counteracting the misstatements of the troubles on the Border, by some of the solid journals of New York. I have nothing to gain, but everything to lose, in making the statements which are embraced in this volume. I do not, I think, array myself in opposition to the sentiment of my brethren in the ministry in this particular. I know that many of them agree with me; in truth, none with whom I have conversed, have intimated a doubt to me that my story was not strictly correct; they lamented such a state of things, but the

question with them is, how they should interest them·
selves to correct the abuses of which I complain.   They
must be their own judges, I am not their master.   But
I have seen men banded together for the prosecution
of highly criminal acts; I have seen these acts carried
into effect by bad men; I have heard worse things advised than it has been possible to carry out.   I have
seen the laws of humanity violated by our own people
against each other, and no notice taken of the affair
by the Government, which acts, if they had been perpetrated by the barbarians of Japan, or the Hottentots
of Africa, upon any of our commercial marine, a
squadron would have been despatched, and sudden vengeance would have fallen on their devoted
heads.

Kansas has been, and is now, in a state of civil war,
and no effort has been made to stop it.   The evil which
keeps the country in its dreadful state of anarchy, is the
outrageous code of laws which has been forced upon the
people by a foreign State, decidedly against the will of
the majority of the residents of the Territory.   I feel
satisfied that those who have read the foregoing pages
will not be so silly as to believe that the troubles began
with the organization of companies of emigration in
Massachusetts.   Every step had been taken to establish
Slavery in Kansas long before the Emigrant Aid Society
had been heard of.   The organization of this Society
startled the Slavery extensionists on the Border.   Of this
there is not the slightest doubt.   But that the Aid Society
had done a great evil, which required retaliation at the
hands of the Pro-Slavery men, is simply absurd.   Long-

cherished plans, of the execution of which there seemed to be no doubt, were put in jeopardy by the organization of the Emigrant Aid Society; and this reflection exasperated the Borderers. I am not the apologist of this Society. One of its chief managers asked me, at Saratoga, to become interested actively in its affairs; I declined, for obvious reasons; but I never doubted that the organization was legitimate, and its operations in the main just and honorable.

Appeals were made from the beginning, to the South by the papers in the Pro-Slavery interest on the Border, to send on men to settle Kansas. The leaders of the party had every hope of the result being in their favor, until steamboat after steamboat landed at Kansas City their loads of Free State settlers. Every day the cry would go up, in the streets of Weston, " Another crew of Abolitionists landed at Kansas!"

These immigrants came peaceably-disposed, as a body. It would have been folly, if not madness, to have come up the Missouri, " vowing vengeance, abolition, and servile insurrection." It cannot be shown that at any one time more than one hundred men in a company ever ascended the Missouri under the auspices of the Aid Society. Just fancy, reader, the attitude of these men in a strange and wild country, on board of a boat belonging to Missourians, setting at defiance the State of Missouri and the United States!

The Missourians saw no enemy and found no enemy in these men. But they did discover that Slavery would not be permitted in Kansas if such men were to be multiplied.

These immigrants, in the main, settled at Law-rence and in its neighborhood. They possessed the whole power there, and acted as law-abiding men, when there was no law in the Territory, and when others were violating the laws of a common humanity.

There were three Free State papers published at Lawrence, "The Herald of Freedom," "The Free State," and the "Tribune." Let any impartial man compare the editorials of these journals with those of the "Leavenworth Herald," the "Squatter Sovereign," and the "Kansas Pioneer;" he will find that while the one party appealed to reason, to common sense, and to the sense of self-preservation, the other inflamed the multitude by arguments addressed to their baser nature. Murder and hanging mingled in every editorial, from the very first issue, and continue to mingle, unto this hour.

Is there on record a single act of barbarity commit-ted by the people of Lawrence during their day of un-doubted power? Not one. I have shown many on the part of the Slave interest. Base, inhuman mur-ders were committed, and no redress could be had by the Free State party.

I never saw Governor Shannon; he had arrived in the Territory about the time I left it. It was the gene-ral impression that he would be a man after the Pro-Slavery party's own heart. And to the best of my knowledge of the state of affairs in that country since, this impression has not been effaced.

He was told to beware of the rock on which Reeder

made shipwreck—the rock *impartiality*. He profited by the warning. He sealed the bloody code, in the blood of honorable American citizens. Those acts for which our fathers were called patriots—the resistance of an odious tyranny—our brethren in Kansas imitated —and by the Government of this Republic they were arrested for Treason; the cannon turned on their dwellings; the public houses, the homes of the stranger, were destroyed, petty thefts committed by the Legal Mob, which ought to have consigned them to the Tombs.

The present condition of the Free State settlers in Kansas is truly alarming. The Code of Blood remains unrepealed. The Missouri laws are in full force. The Executive has determined that they shall be enforced. It is, in my opinion, madness for that noble band of Spartans to remain in that country and be shot down by a legalized mob. There is no mercy there, there is no justice there, for them. The country at large takes no interest in their wrongs. If they remain there in arms against the Government, they must inevitably perish. The Government is a government of a party— it has laid itself at the feet of the Slave power. Let these spirits of freedom come back among us—let them exhibit their rags and wretchedness, their wan coun tenances, their wounds and their bruises—and let the widows and the orphans of the heroes departed, tell us of their wrongs; infinitely more good will be accom- plished, than to remain there to pour out their life- blood for an unattainable good. The Government and the nation are against them.

O justice, thou hast fled to brutish beasts, and men have lost their reason!

" Can no prayers Pierce thee ?"

" Thou almost mak'st me waver in my faith,
To hold opinion with Pythagoras,
That souls of animals infuse themselves
Into the trunks of men ; thy currish spirit
Govern'd a wolf, who, hang'd for human slaughter
Even from the gallows did his fell soul fleet,
And whilst thou lay'st in thy unhallowed dam,
Infused itself in thee ; for thy desires
Are wolfish, bloody, starv'd, and ravenous."

CHAPTER XXXVIII.

TERRITORIAL OFFICERS.

"Twelve butchers for a jury, and a Jeffries for a judge."

WHILE this work has been going through the press, I have been questioned about the Chief Justice of the Territory, and the Marshal of the Territory. I met with these gentlemen at a time when it was supposed that Fort Leavenworth would become the seat of Government; but I did not follow them to the Shawnee Mission, or to Lecompton, the theatre of their chief exploits. The Chief Justice is small of stature, very fair complexion, with quite an intellectual expression of countenance. In Baltimore, where the Judge, I believe, formerly resided, he would, I think, have made a favorable impression; but on the Border men have a faculty of losing their dignity, almost without exception. I think that "model of deportment," Mr. Turveydrop, would have retired in disgust from Kansas.

I have seen the Chief Justice sitting, where better men had sat before him, on a box, in that general rendezvous, the Sutler's office, at Fort Leavenworth; and I have heard him talk as a partisan on Kansas affairs, in such a strain as pot-house politicians would have relished. His construction of the Law suits his humor ·

"Affection,
Mistress of passion, sways it to the mood
Of what it likes, or loaths."

The butchers can at any time be impanelled for a jury, and the modern Jeffries will sit as judge of the Law, and command innocent men to be smitten contrary to the Law.

Marshal Donaldson came from Ohio to Kansas. He is about sixty years of age, perhaps; and the *better* days of his life are not spent in Kansas. He is quite tall tall and slender. He must have been quite anxious to obtain office. He *needed* it, like many of us. He could make himself quite agreeable in every society to be *met with* on the Border. My impression is that he saw the storm rising, when he first reached the territory; but he did not, to my knowledge, define his position until after the Legislature had met and made laws; and, until he found that Reeder's impartiality was rewarded by removal from office; then the Marshal became alarmed; and has ever since been all that could be desired by the "Self-Defensives." "Free State settlers" have been hunted by him as were the Seminole Indians, in Florida, by our army. Extermination, or the most abject submission, was the order in the camp of the Marshal.

CHAPTER XXXIX.

OUR COUNTRY.

In 1850, after the settlement, as it was considered, of the difficulties attending the discussion of the Slavery question, a doctor of divinity in our Episcopal Church, of transcendent abilities, and of oratorical powers not surpassed in the nation, preached a Sermon on the " Union" in our chief city.* It was justly regarded as a great and patriotic effort,—but the most singular mystery connected with the whole affair, is how the great magician could take the " Union" for his text and not preach a *political* sermon!

That the great man did not preach on political subjects is most evident; he was not taken to task or abused in our church papers at the time; neither did the more than pious secular press warn the doctor of the danger, the impropriety, and the awful responsibility of dragging politics into the pulpit! Why, you simpleton, the passage of a " Fugitive Slave Bill" was effected at that crisis; " The Union" was made a hunting ground for runaway negroes, and was this not a subject worthy of prayer, preaching and thanksgiving? Call you that politics? Why, no.

* The preacher was invited to re-deliver the sermon in Washington, which request was complied with, and I believe the Representatives' Hall was thrown open for the purpose

10

Many a time have I said that I would walk ten miles to hear the divine I allude to preach, I so much admired his inimitable manner; he possesses the *ars celare artem* to perfection: but if the magic skill which must have guided his pen while he composed a sermon on the text, "Union," and at the same time kept it free from politics, is to be purchased at any sacrifice in my power, while I compose a sermon on the text, "Our Country," and yet have no political bearing, then let me know what that sacrifice is to be? Name it! At what sacrifice can I obtain the superhuman power?

Oh, Nature, thou hast not been kind to me! Whatever I write or say is taken by the mass of men to mean pretty nearly what my words declare, according to their dictionary definitions; while polished rhetoricians lecture on the Moon, and the press generally report the effort to have been a profound disquisition on "green cheese!"

"Our Country" is my text for a farewell discourse. Is the theme too great for a priest? Is the history of our country written in hieroglyphics? No; but if it were, in all probability you would call on a priest to interpret. Confucius was not our lawgiver; but if he had been, a priest would have as good an opportunity to catch the spirit of the philosopher as any pot-house politician. The Constitution and the Laws of our country are written in plain English, and why may not a priest understand them so as to give an opinion without committing treason? Beardless youths mount the tripod to indite their leaders on Constitutional Law—

it is their legitimate province—read, mark, and learn wisdom! But you, priests, keep out of the arena, dabble not in the filthy pool of politics. The layman has successfully battled with the divine for the right of private judgment in the interpretation of the " Higher Law;" the divine has an opportunity now to show that he may possibly be able to lead a layman to acknowledge that there is a responsibility attaching to the skirts of the gown in the tremendous issues which now involve the honor, the happiness, and the stability of " Our Country."

The honor of our country is involved in the nature of our legislation on the question of human Slavery. The African Slave-trade is piracy, according to our laws. This is well; but is the law founded on just principles? If the law was not in our Statute Book, would the African Slave-trade be piracy according to the law of nature? If we should find savage princes willing to sell what they had stolen, or captured in battle, have we not a right to buy and sell again? The law declares that this trade is piracy, to be punished by death. The law is founded on the right of man to his liberty, and to his own life, and the profits of his own labor. In addition to this principle of right, civilized men have been induced to arrive at this conclusion, by taking a higher and a holier view of the destiny of man, than that arrived at by barbarians. " God has made of one blood all the families of men to dwell on the face of this earth,"—the origin of man is one, his destiny is the same.

The evils which attend the African Slave-trade is

not the basis on which it is declared piracy. If I am not mistaken very much, our Statute unwittingly entails evils which cannot be mentioned without horror, upon the poor victims of man's vile cupidity, such as would not befall them if the traffic were legitimate.

It is generally acknowledged that the means which must be resorted to by the pirates and man-stealers to conceal from our coasters their cargoes of human beings, induce sufferings and woes unparalleled.

Slavery in the United States has no more solid a basis on principle, than has the African Slave-trade. It exists by law, and is tolerated as an evil. It exists as a means of gain. It is tolerated as a means of gain. Negroes are raised for market as a means of gain. The internal Slave-trade is carried on as a means of gain. The existence of the institution itself is wrong, and the attendant and inseparable evils are highly immoral. Everything connected with the institution is a disgrace and a dishonor to the nation. I maintain that this sentiment obtains at the South. The existence of Slavery is lamented, and yet cherished. It is lamented by good men and eschewed by good men. It is lamented by the Slaveholder, while it is cherished by him, and he takes every advantage which the law permits, to make slavery a grievous burden. It is lamented as a debauché laments the propensity to sin which he gives himself no trouble to overcome "The dog returns to his vomit again, and the sow that was washed to her wallowing in the mire."

Is it not sufficient to ask of good men to tolerate

this evil, without insisting upon them to become its patrons and friends?

Freemen, patriots, good and true men, both North and South, the honor of your country is involved. Come to the rescue—tolerate, but never extend this evil! This is the advice which the great departed has left to you—heed it, and live in honor; despise it, and perish in shame!

The happiness of "Our Country," who does not desire? Our happiness depends on our peace and prosperity as a nation.

The energies which are wasted and lost in the angry debates on the subject of Slavery, both in the Congress of the nation, and in the many thousand assemblages of the people—to say nothing of the vast sums expended by the government, and by the people in a private disbursement—would, if turned to the accomplishment of plans for public improvement, explorations of unknown regions of our country, or of the world, the education of our people, the wise regulation of commerce, the humane, and prudent, and beneficent encouragement of immigration, the more efficacious and more just management of the public domain, the amelioration of the condition of the victims of crime and sensuality—finally, the extension of the blessings of the Gospel to those who never heard of the balm for every ill—then our country would more than realize the picture of a happy land, heretofore only painted by the imagination of the poets.

But if Slavery extension is to tax our energies and monopolize the attention of our public men and our

private citizens, and even draw off the minds of ministers of God from more sacred things, then peace and
prosperity, the greatest of earthly blessings, will be
sought for in vain by us.

It is folly to hope that while Slavery is fostered and
extended, and its pathway to Empire cleared by those
in power, that there can be peace or happiness among
our people. There is nothing in the system which
invites a scrutiny that can satisfy or please our minds.
It cannot enlist our pride, or our enthusiasm, or our
love. To ask good Christian men to keep quiet, when
barbarism, in one of its most revolting features, is commanding the attention of a nation like ours, to make
it the very corner-stone of our Institutions, is the extreme of insult; and to go beyond this, and abuse the
ministry of peace and love and purity, because it will
not acquiesce in a plan for the undoing of all the good
which has been accomplished by eighteen centuries of
patient endurance and self-sacrifice in the path of justice and humanity, is putting the seal to our deeds of
impiety.

If it is to become the settled policy of the nation to
throw every new Territory open to adventurers (as
we throw bones to dogs), and encourage these to murder each other on the specious pretext that this is one
of their privileges, while the Slavery question alone is
the point in dispute, then where is peace, and where is
happiness? There is no peace now, and he is crazy who
promises peace in the future. The same bloody scenes
will be enacted as have disgraced our country within
the past two years in Kansas. The answer which is

given to this is, "the principle is right; the theory of the Kansas Bill is good, and in accordance with the spirit of Democracy." It is the duty of every good government to rule the people well. The theory of the Kansas Bill on the subject of Slavery, is nothing but theory; it is not based on just principles; it permits a thoughtless band, not one in a hundred of whom owns a slave, or if owning never considering the evils of Slavery, to go by force and entail unnumbered woes upon a thousand generations who are to inhabit the soil. I could fill a book with the declarations of Southern statesmen wherein this sentiment is endorsed; but what would they amount to? When they made the declarations, it was the wise custom to regard Slavery as a crying evil, if not a daring sin; but now it is one of the recognized subjects for the adoption or rejection of "Squatter Sovereigns," a matter of as little concern as the question whether they shall plow with horses or with oxen.

A Christian people must interfere in this matter, or peace and happiness will take their flight from our Border. The stability of "Our Country," and by this I mean the "Union" of these States in harmony and love—this boon is to be secured permanently by returning to first principles. Refer to the compact by which these States were united. Do we find the least intimation that Slavery is to go *pari passu* with Freedom in the formation of every new State government? or that a balance of power is to be preserved between the Slave and the Free States? Not a word of it. The terms of agreement between the States were very analogous to a firm going into partnership under the following circumstances:

A., B. and C., had all been employed heretofore in a general producing and furnishing business, and among other items, the raising of negroes, and the buying and selling of men. A. was largely in the business; B. moderately engaged; and C. had a few for use at home, but none for sale. They all agreed that this feature in their business did them little good, and reflected no honor; still, their capital was invested, and if a closer partnership was to be made between the parties, the article of human bondage and traffic in men must be tolerated until such times as the article 'would sell off, or die off, and the business close on terms agreeable to A. and B. The partnership was entered into on these terms. For several years everything went on well. C. got rid of his negroes, and B. was in a fair way to get rid of his; but A. found his becoming more and more valuable, and several times threatened to dissolve the partnership, if the terms were not modified on which he went into the firm! A most unreasonable fellow became A.! He saw an enemy in every servant of the establishment, and in pretty much every customer; and a furious fight would he have over every junior partner which might seek for admission into the firm. He forever talked of justice, and the right in the abstract. He acknowledged at one time, that the article for which he claimed the right to engage in more fully, and to take in more stock, was, at the time when the compact was made, unprofitable in a pecuniary point of view, and discreditable in the eyes of mankind; but now he claimed that the market had changed and the current had set for a profitable investment; and that as to the moral sentiment which pervaded mankind, it would also be changed altogether finally, and was in a fair way to be accomplished soon.

> " What makes all doctrines plain and clear ?
> About two hundred pounds a year !
> And that which seemed quite plain before,
> Proved false again?   Two hundred more !"

A. silenced, if he did not convince, B. and C. B. finally determined to hold on to his few negroes and raise stock for A., while both laughed in their sleeve at the wealthy, powerful, but too easy and good-natured old fogy C.   Every servant in the establishment must now be sound on the great question of Slavery-fostering and Slavery-extension, or take his passports.

A. and B. quote no passages from the original compact of the partnership but that clause having reference to giving back the runaways ; while the well-paid servants of the house draw up bills designed to permit of every partner henceforth seeking for admission, to come with a resolute will to sustain and to extend that part of their business which is called slavery and negro-raising, to the subordination of every other item of trade and merchandise.   In addition to all this, the needy clerks draw up documents, technically called *platforms*, on which the man selected to manage the concern is to be laid, promising to forget and ignore all that he had ever said or written, or thought against the propriety of slavery being made the chief article of
10*

trade by the firm. This managing clerk must allow his brains to be extracted, his heart taken out, and his conscience stifled, and permit himself to be placed on the chair at the chief bureau of the firm, a mere automaton, so ghostly and so lifeless that his old servant would not know him.

Is "Our Country's" keeping to be given over to this nameless skeleton? No longer a man, but a platform, on which 340,000 Slaveholders are to crowd; and in their eagerness to whip in and govern twenty millions of people, the bones of the old platform will be ground to powder, and the country ruined! A patriot desires not this state of things; he ought not, therefore, to run the risk. Insist upon the carrying out of the original terms of partnership. There is neither dishonor nor danger in so doing.

There is another platform, whose supporters incline to coquette with Slavery and save the Union. It allows itself, in one section of the country, to be fondled by Slavery, and to throw itself into the hands of Slavery. And while it does this, it would disfranchise several hundred thousand American citizens, as true to the Union and the welfare of this nation as if they had drawn their first breath on its soil. It would make a cipher of a people who have fought and bled for the country—who are the natural enemies of the foes of this Union. This party's platform would rivet the chains of Slavery on the black man forever, and it would enslave the white man who has fled to our shores as a refuge from tyranny and beggary. The peace, the happiness, the prosperity, and the stability of "Our Country" cannot be secured by this organization, and its wisest men have deserted the camp, in despair of ever accomplishing them by such means.

I can find but one party—the party of the honest masses of the people, for whose success I can pray and act, in order to secure the stability of the Union and the peace of the country, and the freedom of that much-abused territory—Kansas. This is the organization which, in honor to the country, asks for the carrying out of the original compact by which this confederacy was founded. No more Slave States founded this Union,—no more Slavery-extension must preserve this Union. This party will respect the rights originally conceded to the South, and all the South ever asked or ever expected to have, when the Union was formed. But it declares boldly that the domain of Freedom shall not be clutched by Slavery. It declares that the power of this Government shall not be used to extend a remnant of barbarism by force and fraud. It declares, more than this, that barbarism shall not be extended farther by us as a Christian people. What good man is there who will not say that these are desirable things? Have them accomplished, then.

There is but one organization pledged to secure these blessings. There is but one organization which will endeavor to secure them. This organization cannot be defeated but by a betrayal of Freedom on the part of those who profess to be Freedom's friends. This is absolutely true. If Freedom is to be crushed to the earth, Kansas ruined, and Slavery-extension made the prime object of the Government, then it will all be accomplished by the North. No good man can, like Gallio, "care for none of these things." Rouse, then, to the salvation of your country. There is a reserve corps in the northern section of our country, which must be called out on the present occasion. It will be found that nearly one-third of those entitled to the elective franchise in the northern States despise it by not exercising it. Look at the census reports, and see if this is not true. This reserve corps is the "Forlorn Hope" of Freedom. Let it be brought forward, and an honorable peace will reward an honorable and a glorious victory. "The Union will then stand." And this reserve corps—this "forlorn hope" of Freedom, will be found among the honest yeomen of the country. Of this I feel well assured. Let, then, the true statement of my experience on the Kansas Border warn you of the designs of the Slave power. It seeks empire. It wishes to beat down the liberty of speech, of the press, and particularly of the pulpit —whose moral power it dreads.

Shall the Protestant Episcopal Church, which boasts of its catholicity—which would pride itself on its anxiety to preach the Gospel to the poor—which cherishes the declaration of St. Paul : "For there is neither Jew nor Greek, Barbarian nor Scythian, Bond nor Free; but Christ is all, and in All"—shall this Church surrender her prerogative to send her ministers to preach the Gospel of Christ anywhere in this Union, no matter what may be their opinion on the subject of Slavery?

It would be criminal for any body of men to make

a law, declaring it to be treason to hold an opinion that African Slavery, in America, is not morally, socially, and politically an evil.

The writer holds this opinion, and yet he is not an Abolitionist; neither will he ever become such, until such times as the evil of Slavery can be done away —moderately, justly, and mercifully. This is the sentiment of the Northern people who think. This is the sentiment of Northern Churchmen; and the day is coming when they must declare themselves openly before the world, or submit to surrender their civil and religious liberties.

The foolish cry of Abolitionism should deter no good man from doing his obvious duty.

Who fears abolition? The South? What reason has the South to fear it? Has it ever been attempted by the interference of an armed mob? Do not cry, then before you are hurt. There are a few negro thieves, as there are other kinds of thieves, and they must operate in the same way, to succeed—by stealth and in secret; but abolition has never been attempted in any illegal manner.

If there are men who are Abolitionists—and I do not deny that there are—your Kansas-Nebraska Bill, and your Slavery-extension measures, have multiplied them ten thousand fold. But the sword has not been taken in hand yet. No Northern mob has invaded your borders. No band of pirates has outraged your ballot-box.

Can Slavery-extensionists say as much good of their friends?

The blood of Kansas freemen cries—No! Widows and orphans of murdered Americans weep, and say—No! The bloody code of Kansas will forever cry—No!

The bought-up cohort of Slavery-extensionists frighten men with the cry of abolition—it disturbs not my nerves. I know that their design is to hold up the country to sale. The empire of Rome was sold and bought; civil wars, as a consequence, deluged it in blood. Republics can be sold and bought again. I can imagine 340,000 slaveholders bidding for a Republic, and I can fancy it betrayed into their hands once, and the experiment tried again. I can see a Marius, and a Scylla, and a Cæsar, and a Pompey, contending for dominion and glory, to be obtained by the ruin of their country. Human nature is not changed; neither has my residence on the Border satisfied me that men have become more civilized than they were in the days of Greek and Roman fame. If dire necessity forces the issue, I presume that even good men would choose the wager of battle, rather than that, by sword and outrage, the moral pestilence of Slavery should be forced upon the unwilling people of many more territories.

Let the Ballot-Box first, and wise Legislation afterwards, stay the advance of Slavery.

Let Freemen exercise their undoubted power and their unquestioned right, in the coming struggle, and then the Upas-tree of Slavery shall not be planted on the fair plains of Kansas, under the shade of which

All death lives, and all life dies."

APPENDIX.

THE writer, in the body of the work, attempted to paint the portrait of the Author of the Black Law; it will be an additional satisfaction to the reader to possess the Bloody Statute itself in a permanent form. It may be important for reference—that he may know why arrests have been made for Treason in Kansas—murders committed there—property destroyed there, by the United States Army, in endeavoring to enforce this law. The reader will also perceive that I was a Traitor in Kansas—that every man who is opposed to Slavery, and residing there, is a Traitor—and that every emigrant, who goes from the East to settle in Kansas, will become a Traitor. More blood is to flow in the enforcing of this law, for the end is not yet.

In addition to the Black Law of my friend, W. P. R., you will find a few extracts from other Model Republican Statutes. The quotations are made from the "Laws of the Territory of Kansas," published by authority of Congress.

CHAPTER 151.—SLAVES.

An Act to Punish Offences against Slave Property.

Be it enacted by the Governor and Legislative Assembly of the Territory of Kansas, as follows:

SECTION 1. That every person, bond or free, who shall be convicted of actually raising a rebellion or insurrection of slaves, free negroes, or mulattoes, in this Territory, shall suffer death.

SEC. 2. Every free person who shall aid or assist in any rebellion or insurrection of slaves, free negroes, or mulattoes, or shall furnish arms, or do any overt act in furtherance of such rebellion or insurrection, shall suffer death.

SEC. 3. If any free person shall, by speaking, writing, or printing, advise, persuade, or induce any slaves to rebel, conspire against, or murder any citizen of this Territory, or shall bring into, print, write, publish, or circulate, or cause to be brought into, printed, written, published, or circulated, or shall knowingly aid or assist in the bringing into, printing, writing, publishing, or circulating in this Territory, any book, paper, magazine, pamphlet, or circular, for the purpose of exciting insurrection, rebellion, revolt, or conspiracy on the part of the slaves, free negroes, or mulattoes, against the citizens of the Territory or any part of them, such person shall be guilty of felony, and shall suffer death.

SEC. 4. If any person shall entice, decoy, or carry away out of this Territory, any slave belonging to another, with intent to deprive the owner thereof of the services of such slave, or with intent to effect or procure the freedom of such slave, he shall be adjudged guilty of grand larceny, and, on conviction thereof, shall suffer death, or be imprisoned at hard labor for not less than ten years.

SEC. 5. If any person shall aid or assist in enticing, decoying, or persuading, or carrying away, or sending out of this Territory, any slave belonging to another, with intent to procure or effect the freedom of such slave, or with intent to deprive the owner thereof or the services of such slave, he shall be adjudged guilty of grand larceny, and, on conviction thereof, shall suffer death, or be imprisoned at hard labor for not less than ten years.

SEC. 6. If any person shall entice, decoy, or carry away out of any State or other Territory of the United States, any slave belonging to another, with intent to procure or effect the freedom of such slave, or to deprive the owner thereof of the services of such slave, and shall bring such slave into this Territory, he shall be adjudged guilty of grand larceny, in the same manner as if such slave had been enticed, decoyed, or carried away out of this Territory, and in such case the larceny may be charged to have been committed in any county of this Territory, into or through which such slave shall have been brought by such person, and on conviction thereof, the person offending SHALL SUFFER DEATH, or be imprisoned at hard labor for not less than ten years.

SEC. 7. If any person shall entice, persuade, or induce any slave to escape from the service of his master or owner, in this Territory, or shall aid or assist any slave in escaping from the service of his master or owner, or shall, aid, assist, harbor, or conceal any slave who may have escaped from the service of his master or owner, he shall be deemed guilty of felony, and punished by imprisonment at hard labor for a term of not less than five years.

SEC. 8. If any person in this Territory shall aid or assist, harbor or conceal, any slave who has escaped from the service of his master or owner, in another State or Territory, such person shall be punished in like manner as if such slave had escaped from the service of his master or owner in this Territory.

SEC. 9. If any person shall resist any officer while attempting to arrest any slave that may have escaped from the service of his master or owner, or shall rescue such slave when in the custody of any officer or other person, or shall entice, persuade, aid or assist such slave to escape from the custody of any officer or other person, who may have such slave in custody, whether such slave have escaped from the service of his master or owner in this Territory, or in any other State or Territory, the person so offending shall be guilty of felony, and punished by imprisonment at hard labor for a term of not less than two years.

SEC. 10. If any marshal, sheriff, or constable, or the deputy of any such officer, shall, when required by any person, refuse to aid or assist in the arrest and capture of any slave that may have escaped from the service of his master or owner, whether such slave shall have escaped from his master or owner in this Territory, or any State or other Territory, such officer shall be fined in a sum of not less than one hundred, nor more than five hundred dollars.

SEC. 11. If any person print, write, introduce into, publish, or circulate, or cause to be brought into, printed, written, published, or circulated, or shall knowingly aid or assist in bringing into, printing, publishing, or circulating within this Territory, any book, paper, pamphlet, magazine, handbill, or circular, containing any statements, arguments, opinions, sentiment, doctrine, advice, or inuendo, calculated to produce a disorderly, dangerous, or rebellious disaffection among the slaves in this Territory, or to induce such slaves to escape from the service of their masters, or to resist their authority, he shall be guilty of felony, and be punished by imprisonment and hard labor for a term of not less than five years.

SEC. 12. If any free person, by speaking or by writing, assert or maintain that persons have not the right to hold slaves in this Territory, or shall introduce into this Territory, print, publish, write, circulate, or cause to be introduced into this Territory, written, printed, published, or circulated in this Territory, any book, paper, magazine, pamphlet, or circular, containing any denial of the right of persons to hold slaves in this Territory, such person shall be deemed guilty of felony, and punished by imprisonment at hard labor for a term of not less than two years.

SEC. 13. No person who is conscientiously opposed to holding slaves, or who does not admit the right to hold slaves in this Territory, shall sit as a juror on the trial of any prosecution for any violation of any of the sections of this act.

This act to take effect, and be in force, from and after the fifteenth day of September, A. D., 1855.

QUALIFICATIONS OF ELECTORS TEST OATHS.

"An Act to regulate Elections" contains the following sections, page 282, chap. 66 :

SEC. 11. Every free white male citizen of the United States, and every free male Indian, who is made a citizen, by treaty or otherwise, and over the age of twenty-one years, who shall be an inhabitant of this Territory, and of the county or district in which he offers to vote, and shall have paid a territorial tax, shall be a qualified elector for all elective officers ; and all Indians who are inhabitants of this Territory, and who may have adopted the customs of the white man, and who are liable to pay taxes, shall be deemed citizens : *Provided*, That no soldier, seaman, or mariner, in the regular army or navy of the United States, shall be entitled to vote, by reason of being on service therein : *And provided further*, That no person who shall have been convicted of any violation of any provision of an act of Congress, entitled, " An act respecting fugitives from justice, and persons escaping from the service of their masters," approved February 12, 1793 ; or of an act to amend and supplementary to said act, approved 18th September, 1850 ; whether such conviction were by criminal proceeding or by civil action for the recovery of any penalty prescribed by either of said acts, in any courts of the United States or of any State or Territory, or of any offence deemed infamous, shall be entitled to vote at any election, or to hold any office in this Territory : *And provided further*, That if any person offering to vote shall be challenged, and required to take an oath or affirmation, to be administered by one of the judges of the election, that he will sustain the provisions of the above-recited acts of Congress, and of the act entitled, " An act to organize the Territories of Nebraska and Kansas," approved May 30, 1854, and shall refuse to take such oath or affirmation, the vote of such person shall be rejected.

Sec. 12. Every person possessing the qualification of a voter, as hereinabove prescribed, and who shall have resided in this Territory thirty days prior to the election, at which he may offer himself as a candidate, shall be eligible as a delegate to the House of Representatives of the United States, to either branch of the legislative assembly, and to all other offices in this Territory, not otherwise especially provided for : *Provided, however*, That each member of the legislative assembly, and every officer elected or appointed to office under the laws of this Territory, shall, in addition to the oath or affirmation specially provided to be taken by such officer, take an oath or affirmation to support the Constitution of the United States, the provisions of an act entitled " An act respecting fugitives from justice, and persons escaping from the service of their masters," approved February 12, 1793 ; and of an act to amend and supplementary to said last-mentioned act, approved September 18, 1850 ; and of an act entitled " An act to organize the Territories of Nebraska and Kansas," approved May 30, 1854.

Sec. 19. Whenever any person shall offer to vote, he shall be presumed to be entitled to vote.

Sec. 20. Whenever any person offers to vote, his vote may be challenged by one of the judges or by any voter, and the judges of the election may examine him touching his right to vote ; and if so examined, no evidence to contradict shall be received. Or the judges may, in the first instance, receive other evidence; in which event, the applicant may if he desire it, demand to be sworn, but his testimony shall not then be conclusive.

Again, on page 438, in Chap. 117, "*An Act regulating oaths, and prescribing the form of oaths of office,*" the following enactments may be found :

SECTION 1. All officers elected or appointed under any existing or subsequently-enacted laws of this Territory. shall take and subscribe the following oath of office : " I, ——, do solemnly swear upon the holy evangelists of Almighty God, that I will support the Constitution of the United States, and that I will support and sustain the provisions of an act entitled ' An act to organize the Territories of Nebraska and Kansas,' and the provisions of the law of the United States, commonly known as the ' Fugitive Slave Law,' and faithfully and impartially, and to the best of my ability, demean myself in the discharge of my duties in the office of —— ; so help me God."

SEC. 2. Which oath of office shall be endorsed on every commission or certificate of appointment, and may be administered by any person in this Territory authorized to administer oaths.

SEC. 6. All oaths and affirmations alike subject the party who shall falsify them to the pains and penalties of perjury.

ATTORNEYS AT LAW—MORE TEST OATHS.

"*An act concerning attorneys at law,*" Chapter 11, page 118, provides as follows :

SEC. 1. No person shall practice as an attorney or counsellor at law, or solicitor in chancery, in any court of record, unless he be a free white male, and obtain a license from the supreme court, or district court, or some one of the judges thereof, in vacation.

SEC. 3. Every person obtaining a license shall take an oath or affirmation to support the Constitution of the United States, and to support and sustain the provisions of an act entitled " An act to organize the Territories of Nebraska and Kansas," and the provisions of an act commonly known as " The Fugitive Slave Law," and faithfully to demean himself in his practice to the best of his knowledge and ability. A certificate of such oath shall be endorsed on the license.

SEC. 5. If any person shall practice law in any court of record, without being licensed, sworn, and enrolled, he shall be deemed guilty of a contempt of court, and punished as in other cases of contempt.

CRIMES AND PUNISHMENTS.

"*An act concerning crimes and the punishment of offences against the persons of individuals,*" Chapter 48, page 205, provides:

SEC. 5. Homicide shall be deemed excusable when committed by accident or misfortune in either of the following cases : *First*, in lawfully correcting a child, apprentice, servant, or slave, or in doing any other lawful act by lawful means, with usual and ordinary caution, and without unlawful intent ; or, *Second*, in the heat of passion, upon any sudden or sufficient provocation, or upon sudden combat without any undue advantage being taken, and without any dangerous weapon being used, and not done in a cruel and unusual manner.

SEC. 31. If any negro or mulatto shall take away any white female under the age of eighteen years, from her father, mother, guardian, or other person having the legal charge of her person, without their consent, for the purpose of prostitution, concubinage, or marriage with him, or any other negro or mulatto, he shall, on conviction, be sentenced to castration, to be performed under the direction of the sheriff, by some skilful person, and the expense shall be adjusted, taxed, and paid as other costs.

SEC. 43. Every person who shall maliciously, forcibly or fraudulently lead, take or carry away, or decoy, or entice away, any child under the age of twelve years, with intent to detain or conceal such child from its parent, guardian, or other person having the lawful charge of such child, shall, upon conviction, be punished by confinement and hard labor, not exceeding five years, or imprisonment in the county jail not less than six months, or by fine not less than five hundred dollars.

"*An act in relation to the general provisions regulating crimes and punishments,*" provides (pages 252 and 253), as follows :

SEC. 27. If any slave shall commit petit larceny, or shall steal any neat cattle, sheep or hog, or be guilty of any misdemeanor, or other offence punishable under the provisions of this act only by fine or imprisonment in a county jail, or by both such fine and imprisonment, he shall, instead of such punishment, be punished, if a male, by stripes on his bare back not exceeding thirty-nine, or if a female, by imprisonment in a county jail not exceeding twenty-one days, or by stripes not exceeding twenty-one, at the discretion of the justice.

SEC. 28. Every slave charged with the commission of any of the offences specified in the last section, shall be tried in a summary manner before a justice of the peace in the county in which the offence is committed ; and such justice (if a jury is not required, as provided for in the next section) shall hear the evidence, determine the cause, and, on conviction, pronounce sentence, and cause the same to be executed.

Sec. 29. If any slave or his master, in any case cognizable before a justice of the peace, shall require a jury, the justice shall cause such jury to be summoned, sworn, and impanelled, who shall determine the facts, and assess the punishment in case of conviction, and the justice shall enter judgment and cause the same to be executed.

Sec. 34. When any slave shall be convicted of a felony punishable by confinement and hard labor, the court before whom such conviction shall be had shall sentence the offender to receive on his bare back any number of stripes not exceeding thirty-nine.

WHO MAY AND WHO MAY NOT BE JURORS.

The quality of justice which a Free State man might reasonably expect at the hands of a Kansas court, may be surmised from Chap. 92, Secs. 1 and 13, of " *An Act concerning jurors,*" pages 377 and 378, from which it will be seen that instead of drawing jurors by lot, the court may summon a sufficient number, (for summon read " pack,") and that all who question the divinity of Slavery are absolutely excluded from all juries which may be required to consider directly or remotely the question of Slavery.

Sec. 1. All courts before whom jurors are required, may order the marshal, sheriff, or other officer, to summon a sufficient number of jurors.

Sec. 13. No person who is conscientiously opposed to the holding slaves, or who does not admit the right to hold slaves in this Territory, shall be a juror in any cause in which the right to hold any person in slavery is involved, nor in any cause in which any injury done to or committed by any slave is in issue, nor in any criminal proceeding for the violation of any law enacted for the protection of slave property and for the punishment of crimes committed against the right to such property.

HABEAS CORPUS.

"*An Act regulating proceedings on writs of habeas corpus.*"
Chapter 79, article 3, page 345, contains the following :

SEC. 8. No negro or mulatto, held as a slave within this Terri
tory, or lawfully arrested as a fugitive from service from another
State or Territory, shall be discharged, nor shall his right of freedom be had under the provisions of this act.

The foregoing provision, suspending the writ of habeas corpus, is
not only a violation of the Constitution of the United States, but
of the Kansas-Nebraska Act itself, which provides as follows :

" Except also that a writ of error or appeal shall also be allowed
to the Supreme Court of the United States, from the decision of
the said supreme court created by this act, or of any judge thereof,
or of the district courts created by this act, or of any judge thereof,
upon any writ of habeas corpus, involving the question of personal
freedom."

THE CHAIN AND BALL.

The following shows the treatment to which citizens are liable
to be subjected for questioning the right of Border Ruffians to
merchandise in human flesh and blood in the Territory of Kansas.
Read and make your own comments. We copy from " *An act pro-
viding a system of confinement and hard labor,*" Chapter 22, page
146.

SEC. 1. Every keeper of a jail, or other public prison, within this
Territory, is hereby required to cause all convicts who may be confined in the prison of which he is the keeper, under sentence of confinement and hard labor, either on the streets, roads, public build-
ings, or other public works of the Territory, or on some public
works of the county in which such convicts may be imprisoned, or
on private works wherever may be hereinafter specified ; or if there
be no public works of the Territory on which to employ such convicts, or if the county wherein such convicts may be confined have
no public works on which to employ such convicts, then such convicts may be employed on the public works of any other county in

the Territory where there may be work to employ such convicts ; or such convicts may be employed on the public works of any incorporate town or city, within this Territory, either in the county in which such convicts may be confined, or in some other county in the Territory,

SEC. 2. Every person who may be sentenced by any court of competent jurisdiction, under any law in force within this Territory, to punishment by confinement and hard labor, shall be deemed a convict, and shall immediately, under the charge of the keeper of such jail or public prison, or under the charge of such person as the keeper of such jail or public prison may select, be put to hard labor, as in the first section of this act specified ; and such keeper or other person, having charge of such convict, shall cause such convict, while engaged at such labor, to be securely confined by a chain six feet in length, of not less than four-sixteenths nor more than three-eighths of an inch links, with a round ball of iron, of not less than four nor more than six inches in diameter, attached, which chain shall be securely fastened to the ankle of such convict with a strong lock and key ; and such keeper or other person, having charge of such convict, may, if necessary, confine such convict, while so engaged at hard labor, by other chains or other means in his discretion, so as to keep such convict secure and prevent his escape ; and when there shall be two or more convicts under the charge of such keeper, or other person, such convicts shall be fastened together by strong chains, with strong locks and keys, during the time such convicts shall be engaged in hard labor without the walls of any jail or prison.

CPSIA information can be obtained
at www.ICGtesting.com
Printed in the USA
BVHW02s1753201117
500906BV00021B/987/P